Editor-in-Chief and Founder:
  Lyndon H. LaRouche, Jr.
Editorial Board: *Lyndon H. LaRouche, Jr. , Helga
  Zepp-LaRouche, Robert Ingraham, Tony
  Papert, Gerald Rose, Dennis Small, Jeffrey
  Steinberg, William Wertz*
Co-Editors: *Robert Ingraham, Tony Papert*
Managing Editor: *Nancy Spannaus*
Technology: *Marsha Freeman*
Books: *Katherine Notley*
Ebooks: *Richard Burden*
Graphics: *Alan Yue*
Photos: *Stuart Lewis*
Circulation Manager: *Stanley Ezrol*

INTELLIGENCE DIRECTORS
Counterintelligence: *Jeffrey Steinberg, Michele
  Steinberg*
Economics: *John Hoefle, Marcia Merry Baker,
  Paul Gallagher*
History: *Anton Chaitkin*
Ibero-America: *Dennis Small*
Russia and Eastern Europe: *Rachel Douglas*
United States: *Debra Freeman*

INTERNATIONAL BUREAUS
Bogotá: *Miriam Redondo*
Berlin: *Rainer Apel*
Copenhagen: *Tom Gillesberg*
Houston: *Harley Schlanger*
Lima: *Sara Madueño*
Melbourne: *Robert Barwick*
Mexico City: *Gerardo Castilleja Chávez*
New Delhi: *Ramtanu Maitra*
Paris: *Christine Bierre*
Stockholm: *Ulf Sandmark*
United Nations, N.Y.C.: *Leni Rubinstein*
Washington, D.C.: *William Jones*
Wiesbaden: *Göran Haglund*

ON THE WEB
e-mail: eirns@larouchepub.com
www.larouchepub.com
www.executiveintelligencereview.com
www.larouchepub.com/eiw
Webmaster: *John Sigerson*
Assistant Webmaster: *George Hollis*
Editor, Arabic-language edition: *Hussein Askary*

EIR (ISSN 0273-6314) *is published weekly
(50 issues), by EIR News Service, Inc.,
P.O. Box 17390, Washington, D.C. 20041-0390.
(703) 297-8434*

European Headquarters: E.I.R. GmbH, Postfach
Bahnstrasse 9a, D-65205, Wiesbaden, Germany
Tel: 49-611-73650
Homepage: http://www.eir.de
e-mail: info@eir.de
Director: Georg Neudecker

Montreal, Canada: 514-461-1557
eir@eircanada.ca

Denmark: EIR - Danmark, Sankt Knuds Vej 11,
basement left, DK-1903 Frederiksberg, Denmark.
Tel.: +45 35 43 60 40, Fax: +45 35 43 87 57. e-mail:
eirdk@hotmail.com.

Mexico City: EIR, Sor Juana Inés de la Cruz 242-2
Col. Agricultura C.P. 11360
Delegación M. Hidalgo, México D.F.
Tel. (5525) 5318-2301
eirmexico@gmail.com

Copyright: ©2017 EIR News Service. All rights
reserved. Reproduction in whole or in part without
permission strictly prohibited.

Canada Post Publication Sales Agreement
#40683579

Postmaster: Send all address changes to *EIR*, P.O.
Box 17390, Washington, D.C. 20041-0390.

Signed articles in *EIR* represent the views of the authors,
and not necessarily those of the Editorial Board.

Crush 'Maidan II'

THE CHARLOTTESVILLE EVENT

A New Phase of the Coup

by Barbara Boyd

Aug. 16—The "Russiagate" campaign to delegitimize and overthrow the President has been seriously damaged by the revelation that the Russians did not hack the Democratic National Committee. As the Veterans Intelligence Professionals for Sanity published, and as the *Nation* magazine republished, the DNC emails were leaked by an insider, not hacked.

Since then, the American version of the British Color Revolutions conducted internationally, has opened a new front against the President—the all-consuming American wound called the race card. All psychological-warfare operations of this kind are based on population profiles of what seem to be irresolvable problems within the targeted society.

Let us be very clear. There is an outbreak of the purest hypocrisy on this issue now taking place in the United States, with outright genocidalists and eugenicists, such as George H.W. Bush (NSSM 200, Willy Horton, crack cocaine throughout the nation's ghettos), George W. Bush (Mr. Compassionate Conservative, purchaser and destroyer of the African-American clergy, killer of millions), and Larry Summers ("let's dump toxic waste on Africa"), all coming forward to decry the President's alleged moral equivocation on the issue of race.

The President was absolutely correct in implying that this was a staged event for political purposes. He was more than correct when he stated that the only solution to the issue of race in America is productive jobs. That was the point emphasized by Lyndon LaRouche in a report he wrote in the 1970s called "What Ever Happened to Integration?" It is as applicable today as it was when it was written.

Ask yourself whether the business executives now abandoning Trump and proclaiming themselves diversity fiends, have done a damn thing about creating productive jobs in the United States over the last 20 years.

The presidency of Barack Obama, and its equation of identity politics with social progress, created the present caldron in the United States. There was absolutely no economic progress made under Obama's reign—only the flooding of the ghettos with drugs, gangs, and economic despair.

It is standard British counterinsurgency practice to pit ideologically conditioned gangs against one another in an endless cycle of violence and murder, a strategy perfected in the British war against the Mau Mau in Kenya by Brig. General Frank Kitson, and called just that, "gang/countergang."

In the case of Charlottesville, both gangs in the action were either controlled by the FBI or by other trained intelligence operatives on the scene.

The Klan and White Supremers on the scene, Richard Spencer and David Duke, are long-time assets in the FBI orbit. Duke was largely a George H.W. Bush creation.

It turns out that the other major figure, Jason Kessler, now proclaimed to be "Alt Right," was actually an Obama activist until November 2016, and participated heavily in "Occupy Wall Street." Some say he was an assignment editor at that point for CNN. A strange metamorphosis, to say the least. The man who drove the car injuring many and killing a protester, was a mentally ill grifter named James Fields, whose fascination with Nazism and violence had been profiled by authorities since high school.

On the other side are Virginia Governor Terry McAuliffe; Charlottesville Mayor Michael Signer; Brennan Gilmore, a former State Department employee who some say worked for the CIA; the Obama "resist" apparatus in Virginia; and the violent, lawless anarchist grouping known as "Antifa."

The plan to remove the Robert E. Lee statue, and for a large rally to protest it, featuring "White Power" gangs, had been underway for a very, very long time. It is typical of gang/countergang operations now taking place throughout the United States involving Alt-Right provocateurs and Antifa resisters, which have resulted in riots, injuries, and huge property damage in Berkeley, Portland and other locations.

In Charlottesville, the "white" protesters procured a permit after a widely-publicized court fight. Both sides organized extensively through social media. The counter-protesters included the Progressive Change Campaign Committee, Standing Up for Social Justice, Refuse Fascism, Black Lives Matter, and other George Soros-funded and controlled groups, as well as the violent anarchist Antifa. The counter-protest was also widely promoted by the Center for American Progress of John Podesta, which is the institutional center of the anti-Trump "Resist" apparatus.

Immediately after Trump's election, Charlottesville Mayor Michael Signer said that the city would be the capital of the "Resistance" to Donald Trump. At the same time, the main initial social-media organizers of "Indivisible," one of the first anti-Trump internet movements, had migrated to Virginia to run Obama protégé Tom Perriello's campaign for Governor. Perriello had formerly worked for the State Department in Africa. His Virginia campaign was heavily backed by the Center for American Progress. His campaign chief of staff, Brennan Gilmore, was reportedly involved in a Color Revolution in the Central African Republic, pitting Muslims against Christians, and resulting in a subsequent genocide, although we have not yet been able to fully confirm these reports.

Governor Terry McAuliffe's Clintonista political background and propensity for political stunts and sleazy activities are well known. On Friday night, Aug. 11, "white power" racists marched using the same "tiki torches" employed by Neo-Nazis in the British/Obama Color Revolution in Ukraine in 2014.

According to all reports of what happened Saturday, Signer and McAuliffe collaborated to have the police run the two opposing groups together, rather than separating them, and then stood down when violence erupted between the heavily armed factions of both gangs. Perhaps not accidentally, it was Brennan Gilmore who captured the video of Fields' car mowing down the "counter-demonstrators" and killing the young woman, Heather Heyer. It is his video which has been circulated over and over again on television and on the internet.

EIRContents

www.larouchepub.com Volume 44, Number 34, August 25, 2017

Cover This Week

The Maidan in Kiev, Ukraine, 2014.

Race Is Not the Issue

by Robert Ingraham

Aug. 19—Since the moment Donald Trump was sworn in as President, the British and American establishments have been—and continue to be—determined to remove him from office. This has nothing to do with racism, hacked DNC computers, or any other such nonsense. What they fear, and what they are determined to stop, is the President's stated intention to bring about a rapprochement of the United States with Russia and China, an initiative which also portends future U.S. participation in the global Belt and Road Initiative (BRI), the economic development initiative of the Chinese government. This intention, repeatedly stated by Donald Trump, threatens London and Wall Street. It threatens their geopolitical power and their self-appointed right to run the world.

The British empire and that empire's allies within the United States have been explicit: "Trump must go." For months, fraudulent lies about "Russia-gate" have been plastered all over the news media. A Special Prosecutor was appointed based on outright lies. Now those lies have been exposed and discredited by the release of the report by the Veteran Intelligence Professionals for Sanity (VIPS). So a new lie is created: Trump is a racist! The *chutzpah* of this propaganda is mind-boggling.

In the wake of the violence and the death in Charlottesville, Virginia on Aug. 12, Trump has been labeled a "bigot" and a "racist," and an atmosphere has been created in which an assassination of the President could be explained away by his enemies in the news media as a product of "violent emotions" within the population, emo-tions which they, themselves, have worked tirelessly to inflame.

The most stunning fact in the current crisis is that the people who are now hurling charges of racism against Donald Trump are doing so *on behalf of* the same imperial interests who created the global slave system, who created modern racism, and who, over more than four hundred years, murdered tens of millions human beings—as they continue to murder millions today. The slave-drivers and mass-murderers have simply re-written the history books to whitewash their crimes. Today's fools dance to their tune, as if in some perverted minstrel show.

It is time to clear the air. It is time to tell some truths. It is time to place the blame for slavery and America's racial problems squarely on the shoulders of those responsible. It is also time for Americans to grow up, and to cease dealing with the subject of slavery—and all of its ramifications—in the simplistic, juvenile fashion which is promoted in the mass media and Hollywood.

Scene from a British slave ship.

A slave ship.

The Truth

American slavery was created by the British Empire, and the American Revolution was the greatest victory over slavery in the history of the human race. In the 18th Century, the entire world was in the grip of vast European-controlled slave empires. The American Revolution changed that.

Slavery is an oligarchical policy. The motive that drove the British Crown to create a slave empire is identical to what we see today in the financial and economic policies emanating from Wall Street, the City of London, the International Monetary Fund, and the British Monarchy. Their policy is one of looting populations, prohibiting scientific and economic progress, enforcing poverty and backwardness on the majority of the human race, and "culling the herd" through wars, starvation, disease, and drugs, as prescribed by Bertrand Russell.

The idea that slavery or racism is an "American" phenomenon is absurd on the face of it. It is the Big Lie, perpetrated by the same imperial oligarchical interests now intent on saving the usurious London/Wall Street financial system and sabotaging China's Belt and Road development policy. These oligarchs will overthrow governments, impeach Presidents or go to global war to preserve their power.

What follows is a preliminary report. It is presented now, in its incomplete form, to counter the lies and de-lusions that have been circulated in the wake of the events in Charlottesville.

I. Slavery Didn't Start in America

In 1775, as the opening shots of the American Revolution were reverberating, slavery was a world-wide reality. It was widespread and native to India; it was widespread and native in both Russia and China; and it was widespread, internally, throughout Africa. For a period of at least four hundred years, the most pervasive use of slavery, as well as the control over mass African slave-trading, was in the Islamic world, where Muslim traders took millions of slaves out of Africa. By the time of the American Revolution, tens—perhaps hundreds—of millions were enslaved, and slavery existed on every continent, as a feature of oligarchical rule.

Beginning in the mid- to late-15th Century, the Portuguese entered the picture, initiating an escalating involvement of the European empires in the African slave trade. They were soon joined by the Spanish, the Dutch, and the French. Between 1500 and 1880, 12 million Africans were transported across the Atlantic into slavery. Almost all of them were sent to the giant sugar plantations of Brazil (which took a staggering five million slaves), Surinam, Barbados, Cuba, Saint-Domingue, Jamaica and other islands in the Carribean. These were not "colonies"; they were not created for the immigration of free families. These were all commercial enterprises, run directly by the European monarchies and designed to maximize monetary profit for the imperial powers. From the beginning it was the European empires who forced slavery on the New World.

The sugar plantations were scenes of mass murder. Life expectancy in Jamaica or Barbados was *five years, or less,* from the point a slave arrived at the sugar plantation. They were simply worked to death or killed outright if they caused problems. Sex (or marriage) between slaves was strictly prohibited, because it was deemed far cheaper to simply import more slaves from Africa than to incur the expense of raising slave children from infancy. All of these charnel houses were overseen by Royally appointed Governors.

The apex of the trans-Atlantic slave trade was from 1680 to 1808, and it was dominated by the British. In that 128-year span, the British Empire took six million slaves out of Africa, *fully 50%* of the 380-year total. Between 1701 and 1776 the British brought 300,000 of those slaves into the North American colonies, and this was done for the purpose of cloning their slave model from Jamaica and Barbados in the thirteen colonies. The intention was to have all of the colonies based on slave labor.

The North American Colonies

Of the total 12 million slaves who made the trans-Atlantic voyage, only 388,000 were shipped to the thirteen North American colonies, slightly more than three percent of the total. The truth is that the North American colonies, particularly before 1688, were the exception to the British slave model. They were settled by free colonists, with the single exception of South Carolina, which was founded by slave owners from Barbados. Between the founding of the Jamestown colony in 1608, and 1688, *fewer than 15,000* slaves were brought into the colonies, and between 1620 and 1670 there were no laws, in any of the colonies, recognizing or enforcing slavery. During this period, African slaves in the American colonies were treated far differently from those in Brazil or the Caribbean. Most of the colonies granted them similar, or in some cases, equal rights to those of indentured servants—including the right of literacy—and the social standing of the two groups was nearly identical. These rights varied from place to place, but included the right to marry, have children, give testimony in court, sue their owners, hire out their labor, and to purchase their freedom.

The first slaves were brought into the American colonies in 1619, at Jamestown, Virginia, and 1626 in New Amsterdam. Both groups of slaves were brought in by ships of the Dutch West Indies Company, the imperial Dutch company which was created for the single purpose of seizing control over tHe West African slave trade from the Portuguese. Despite Dutch efforts to build up slavery in New Amsterdam, throughout much of the 17th Century, the number of slaves in North America remained relatively small.

This changed after Britain seized control of the African slave trade. In 1660, the British monarchy created the Royal African Company, with the Duke of York—later King James II—as its head. James's immediate goal was to transform New York into the hub for the spread of slavery in the colonies. Between 1672 and 1689, the Company transported 100,000 slaves across the Atlantic, some branded with the letters "DY," for Duke of York, others branded with "RAC," for Royal African Company. This was a top-down policy, designed and implemented at the highest level of imperial power in London. Control over the slave trade was based in the King's Privy Council and the Board of Trade. Then, in 1688, the "Glorious Revolution" brought the Dutch King William to the British throne, and the slave trade was opened to all British merchants. When this was combined with Spain's granting of the *asiento* (the permission to sell slaves in the Spanish colonies) to Britain at the Treaty of Utrecht in 1713, Britain gained hegemony over global slave trafficking.

The floodgates were open. In 1720, there were 39,000 slaves in Virginia and Maryland (the two largest slave-owning colonies) and 5,700 slaves in New York, the northern colony with the most slaves. Yet after a half century of massive British slave-trafficking, there were over 500,000 slaves in the colonies by 1776. In one year, 1768, British ships transported more than 110,000 slaves out of Africa. One of the first actions taken by the British was to redefine slavery as a *race-based* institution. One year after seizing New Amsterdam, in 1665, the Royal AfricAn Company enacted a law in New York which stated that only blacks could be enslaved. Shortly afterward, the Royal Governor of Virginia enacted a similar law. This defining of the question of "freedom or slavery" based on the color of one's skin had been unheard of in the colonies up to that time.

A major inflection point came with Bacon's Rebellion in Virginia in 1676, when whites and blacks joined together in an integrated armed revolt against the oppression of the imperial Royal Governor. In the aftermath of that conflict, first in Virginia, and then later in other colonies, the British rulers imposed a policy of separating the races, removing all previously recognized legal rights of the African slaves, and enforcing a social regimentation which asserted the biological and intellectual inferiority of the black race. Embedded in these actions was a conscious design to *pit the races against each other.*

The slave trade became a torrent, a whirlwind of human suffering and oppression, all directed from London, all on behalf of the Monarchy. At the same time, through a series of trade and navigation acts, together with Royal edicts and regulations from the Board of Trade, by the beginning of the 18th Century, Britain unleashed a process to snuff out the rights of the white colonists: to prohibit, by law, industrial and scientific development, and to reduce the previously free inhabitants of the thirteen colonies to a condition of servitude. By the 1760s, the British Monarchy was determined to impose its "Barbados Model" on all of the American colonies, to transform the entirety of their possessions in the Western hemisphere into slave-based economies. The American Revolution was a war precisely against that future of slavery and subservience.

The Creek Indians meet with James Oglethorpe (standing with hat).

II. The American Anti-Slavery Revolt

The lark of freedom sang in 1775. Free black soldiers fought alongside their white comrades at Lexington, Concord and Bunker Hill. This was a Revolution—an astounding breakthrough for the human species! In 1775, every major European nation possessed a vast slave empire, which they enforced with brutal ruthlessness—killing millions in the process,—and it was in the new United States that liberation began. There is simply no arguing with that self-evident truth.

Prior to 1770, slavery was legal—by Royal decree—in all thirteen British *colonies*; but by 1790 a majority of the now free *states* had either emancipated their slaves or taken steps in that direction, and this momentum was spreading throughout the new nation, including into the South. Nothing like this had ever occurred anywhere in the world, at least not in the modern era.

Benjamin Rush

The Pre-Revolutionary Mindset

From very early, it was clear to many courageous and perceptive Americans that resistance to Britain must include liberty for all of the inhabitants of the colonies, of all races and ethnic and religious backgrounds. As early as 1700, Samuel Sewall, a close ally of Increase and Cotton Mather, and a leader of Old South Church in Boston, authored and published *The Selling of Joseph,* a harsh, uncompromising attack on black slavery, wherein he calls for emancipation of all of the slaves.

In 1733, the colony of Georgia was founded by James Oglethorpe, with a strict ban on slavery. Oglethorpe warned that any introduction of black slaves would "occasion the misery of thousands in Africa." (Unfortunately, Oglethorpe's ban on slavery would be overturned in 1749 by South Carolina planters who emigrated into the new Georgia colony.)

In 1773, Benjamin Rush, later the Treasurer of the U.S. Mint, published *An Address to the Inhabitants of the British Settlements in America, upon Slave-Keeping.* He assailed the slave trade as well as the entire institution of slavery. Rush took direct aim at the British argument that blacks were morally and intellectually inferior. He said that the supposed backwardness of the individual slave was only the perverted expression of slavery, which "is so foreign to the human mind, that the moral faculties, as well as those of the understanding are debased, and rendered torpid by it."

Throughout the 18th Century, the individual colonies made repeated efforts to stop the slaves from coming in. Between 1726 and 1776, the Virginia House of Burgesses passed *twenty-eight* laws to outlaw the importation of slaves into Virginia. They were clear and adamant: "We don't want your slaves." All of these laws were nullified by the Board of Trade and/or the Privy Council. Other colonies issued near-identical laws, and all were overridden by London.

In 1774, John Jay issued an *Address to the People of Great Britain,* charging Britain as acting as "an advocate for slavery and oppression," and the same year, in one of its very first actions, the U.S. Continental Congress banned slave imports and U.S. participation in the Slave Trade.

The Revolution

• 1775: Pennsylvania Abolition Society formed in Philadelphia, the first abolition society within the territory that is now the United States of America.

• 1776: The Declaration of Independence is adopted, with its imperative that "all men are created equal."

• 1777: Vermont abolishes slavery. Gouverneur Morris authors a New York State Constitution which bans slavery, but the emancipation clause is removed by the other delegates.

• 1780: John Jay writes a letter, saying that unless the new nation enacts emancipation of the slaves, the country's "prayers to Heaven will be impious." Pennsylvania abolishes slavery.

• 1782: Virginia enacts a law allowing for private manumission of slaves.

• 1783: Massachusetts and New Hampshire abolish slavery.

• 1785: Founding of the "New York Society for Promoting the Manumission of Slaves, and Protecting Such of Them as Have Been or May Be Liberated." Near passage of an emancipation law in New York; it passed in both houses in different versions, but the differences could not be resolved.

• 1787: Adoption of the Northwest Ordinance, outlawing any new slavery in the Northwest Territories. Creation of the African Free School in New York. At the Constitutional Convention, an effort for the immediate suppression of the slave trade fails by a narrow margin, and Gouverneur Morris attempts to limit the power of the slave states by opposing the Three-Fifths Clause.

• 1788: New York, Massachusetts and Pennsylvania outlaw the slave trade. Legislation to abolish slavery in Delaware fails by one vote.

• 1789: Delaware bans the slave trade.

• 1790: A petition to Congress by Pennsylvania Abolition Society, signed by its President Benjamin Franklin, calls for an end to the slave trade and the freeing of slaves. The Richmond, Virginia Abolition Society is founded.

• 1794: The U.S. Congress passes, and President Washington signs, the Slave Trade Act, banning both American ships from participating in the slave trade, and the importation of slaves by foreign ships.

Gouverneur Morris

portrait by Gilbert Stuart 1820.
Rufus King

- 1799: New York abolishes slavery.
- 1800: American citizens are banned from investment and employment in the international slave trade in an additional Slave Trade Act.
- 1802: The Ohio state constitution abolishes slavery.

Also, between 1776 and 1800 large numbers of slave owners—in both tHe North and South—freed their slaves. There was a drastic decline in the number of slaves and an increase in free blacks in both Maryland and Delaware. The free black population of Maryland was 1,817 in 1755, 20,000 in 1800, and by 1810, a quarter of the state's black population was free. Virginia's free black population rose from 12,866 in 1790 to 30,570 in 1810. There was also a dramatic improvement in legal rights for freed blacks as well as for slaves.

Again, nothing like this had ever been seen anywhere in the world. As America began dismantling the British-created slave system, all of the other colonies of the British Empire, as well as those of Spain, France, the Netherlands and Portugal, continued to operate within the Inferno of a global slave-based paradigm.

The mandarin Li in this painting is ordering the destruction of 20,291 bales of opium. In the face of this opposition to the British East India Company shipments to China, Britain waged the 1839-1842 Opium War and militarily forced China to import the mind-destroying opium.

British clipper ship in Nanjing, China.

The British Respond

Outright fools have bought the line that "civilized" Britain led the way in the abolition of slavery, and the passage of British emancipation in 1834 was long celebrated as a British holiday. Utter, utter, rubbish! It was the victories coming from America, particularly between 1775 and 1797, which dealt the death blow to slavery as a global system, and by 1834—when they had allegedly "seen the light" on slavery—the British Empire had already moved on to the far more lucrative—and more murderous—international drug trade, as the means to expand their monetary wealth and imperial power.

By the end of the 18th Century, the profitability of the African slave trade began to evaporate. The response of Britain was to create a new global trade monopoly, this one based on opium. In 1750, the British East India Company conquered and took control of Bengal and Bihar, the prime opium-growing regions in India. By 1767 they were already shipping 140,000 pounds of opium per year into China. But this was only the beginning. In 1820 the British shipped 595,000 pounds of opium, and this rose to 1.4 million pounds in 1830 and a staggering 5.6 million pounds by 1838. Far more money flowed into London banks from opium trafficking than had ever been realized from the slave trade. Millions died. Tens of millions fell victim to opium addiction, and the City of London financial empire was built on the profits of this mass murder.

At the same time, as the 19th Century American

A slave auction in Virginia, 1861.

economist Henry Carey demonstrated, British imperial policy in both India and Ireland was *de facto* one of mass enslavement and genocide. In his 1853 work, *The Slave Trade Domestic and Foreign,* Carey also irrefutably proves that the conditions then being imposed by Britain on tens of millions in India and Ireland were actually far worse than the condition of slaves in the U.S. South.

In the United States, slavery became a geopolitical pawn for the British, one to be used to disrupt and subvert the new American republic. British banks played a major role in transforming the entire American South into one gigantic, slave-based, cotton economy (much as they did with opium in India). The British also recruited "junior partners" in New England who were used to revive the slave trade. Between 1789 and 1808, these New England merchants brought 100,000 new slaves into the United States, almost entirely into the deep South. The New England slave trade is often cited as proof of "American racism," but isn't this the way that British colonialism has always worked? To buy off and corrupt members of the native aristocracy? Isn't this what was later done in India, in Kenya, in Malaya and elsewhere? These American slave and opium traffickers were "allowed" to operate by the British. They were the "small fry"—given a slice of the profits—and they were cultivated by the British for one reason only, to create a faction in the United States loyal to British financial interests.

The Slave Power Counterattack

In 1801, Thomas Jefferson became President, and for the next twenty-four years Virginia slave-owners, backed by the fanatics from South Carolina and Georgia, ruled the nation. In 1803, South Carolina re-opened its ports to the African slave trade (it had previously been banned in all of the states), and in 1806, Virginia enacted a law forcing all manumitted slaves to leave the state within a year or be re-enslaved. New slave states were created, the Louisiana Territory was opened to slavery, and everywhere legal rights for both slaves and freed blacks were rolled back. The British Carribean plantation system spread through the South. This downward spiral escalated following the War of 1812, and it was accompanied by vicious propaganda alleging the moral and intellectual inferiority of blacks.

The end of the American Revolution's anti-slavery impulse came in 1820 with the passage of the Missouri

The German artist Rugendas depicts a scene below the deck of a slave ship sailing to Brazil, 1830; Rugendas was an eye witness.

Compromise, and it is critical for everyone to recognize the implications of what that action represented. Beginning with the first Continental Congress in 1774 and continuing through the adoption of the United States Constitution, slavery was entirely an institution controlled by the individual states. America was not a "slave nation"; Virginia and the others were "slave states."

The American government did not recognize slavery as a national institution, and national policy was defined by such actions as the Northwest Ordinance and the banning of the trans-Atlantic slave trade. The Missouri Compromise of 1820 did not merely admit Missouri as a slave state; it codified into federal law that all land of the United States below the 36°30′ parallel would now be slave territory. It made slavery a legal feature of the *nation,* and it redefined America as a nation (not just states) where slavery was legal. This was a national catastrophe, as recognized at the time by John Jay and Rufus King.

By mid-century, British and allied "theorists" would create the "sciences" of Social Darwinism, Race Science, and Eugenics, all designed to divide humanity on racial grounds, and all intended to justify the classification of whole sections of the human population as inferior and "sub-human"—and, therefore, expendable. The poison of these "sciences" was then spread by the elite "Ivy League" universities, many of which had been created with money supplied by Britain's junior partners in the slave and opium trades.

III. The Principle of Public Credit

Let us go beyond a mere recitation of history. At this point, let us ask ourselves: What are the underlying Principles involved in this discussion of slavery? What was the real issue of the American Revolution?

The heart and soul of the American Republic is to be found in a series of writings authored by Alexander Hamilton between 1789 and 1791, particularly his *Report on a National Bank,* his *Report on Manufactures,* and his *Opinion as to the Constitutionality of the National Bank.* It is within these writings that Hamilton defines the *Principle of Public Credit* as the basis for the new nation.

What exactly is Public Credit? To answer that question, first return to the specter of human enslavement and oligarchical rule, then hegemonic world wide,

oil portrait by Daniel Huntington.

Alexander Hamilton

during Hamilton's lifetime. The world was run by imperial systems, based on monetarist notions of wealth, in which human beings were mere commodities. Hamilton rejected this. He insisted that the real wealth of a nation lies with the creative potential of each of her citizens. The origins for Hamilton's outlook are to be found in Gottfried Leibniz' *Society and Economy,* and other of his writings, where Leibniz says that all human development flows from new inventions and discoveries in the physical sciences, which increase mankind's "power over nature" and lead to leaps in individual and national productivity. None of this is driven by "market forces" or by the pursuit of monetary profit, but rather, emerges from the creative potentials which exist within each human individual.

What Hamilton created was the power of "Public Credit" or "national credit," whereby that creative human impulse becomes the basis for the future economic development of society as a whole. The intention was to *Uplift the People,* to rescue them from scratching in the dirt like wild animals, and to create a future of progress, where the full human potential might be realized. Money is dead; Public Credit, as Hamilton envisioned it, is alive, it is a *living creative force,* a *vis viva,*—it is a catalyst for investment in those things which will improve the human condition and man's mastery over nature. It is the *Creative Principle,* which marshals the economic, financial, and creative resources of the nation, as a whole, to create new revolutionary potentialities.

Hamilton posited that the nation itself must be based on this Principle. He devised means whereby the economic resources of the nation would be deployed for investments in science, manufacturing and new inventions. And all of this was to be based on a free productive workforce: Citizens, not subjects.

It is self evident that such an approach also defines a very specific definition of the Human Identity and a recognition of the universal creative potentialities which exist within every human being.

It was no accident that Hamilton was a founding member of New York's Manumission Society, nor that after his departure from the Washington Administration, he devoted a great portion of the last decade of his life to the work of that Society. Nor is it a coincidence that Hamilton's closest allies—John Jay, Gouverneur Morris, Rufus King, and others—shared Hamilton's commitment to emancipation, and it was these individuals who made up the leadership of George Washington's eight-year Presidency.

Washington himself was virulently anti-slavery. The slaves he owned were inherited or obtained through marriage, and he freed all of them in his will. His closest confidants, during his Presidency, were the leaders of the emancipation movement. He wrote a letter of congratulations to Hamilton's friend John Laurens for his efforts to free thousands of slaves in South Carolina, and, in 1786, he sent a letter to Lafayette, after Lafayette had purchased a plantation and freed all the slaves, praising him, and saying, "Your late purchase of an estate in the colony of Cayenne, with a view of emancipating the slaves on it, is a generous and noble proof of your humanity. Would to God a like spirit would diffuse itself generally into the minds of the people of this country."

Even though many of the anti-slavery victories achieved by the heroes of the American Revolution were rolled back for a time—much as the victories of the 1867-1876 Reconstruction Era were rolled back—what is crucial is to consider what defines the nature of a Revolution of Principle. Such a revolution is never concluded; it is never finished. Each new generation must create fresh victories. Hamilton designed an approach to human economic and cultural development which has yet to be fully realized. The oligarchical purveyors of slavery and mass murder whom we fought in 1776 still sit in positions of power. It is the task of Hamilton's unfinished Revolution which defines the only sane approach to the issues of "racism" and "slavery" today.

Today's Charlatans

Under Barack Obama, "racism" was redefined, transformed into a bizarre caricature within the realm of "Identity Politics," wherein various ethnic and other groups are self-defined by their level of "oppression." Racism and other "hate crimes" are now viewed as lobotomized "ethical" issues, divorced from any connection to the history of empire and the economic policies of the financial elite. "Don't be a hater," the adolescent wails. This is the drug-induced John Lennon view of peace and human brotherhood.

Most of those now demanding Donald Trump's resignation would not recognize racism or slavery if it bit them on the nose. The most significant step in recent history that has pushed the world in the direction of a new slavery, a new mass murder, was the repeal of Glass-Steagall in 1999. Since that repeal we have lived through almost two decades of unbridled financial looting, growing impoverishment, and escalating death rates. How many Americans make that connection? Anti-Trump activists who are not fighting tooth and nail for the restoration of Glass-Steagall and for the United States to join the Belt and Road Initiative, are frauds, fools, and dupes of British propaganda—and they all stand exposed as understanding *nothing* about slavery or racism.

Franklin Roosevelt was passionately committed to abolishing European colonialism, to building dams, irrigation projects, and railroads, and to bringing electricity to Africa and other impoverished parts of the world. Today, China has taken up that mission, and is uplifting millions through the Belt and Road Initiative. President Trump has expressed interest in joining this process. London and Wall Street say, "No! We reserve the right to prohibit economic development. Our monetary and financial policies shall rule the world." That is the British System. The British Slave System. That is what Alexander Hamilton fought against.

Active LaRouche Principle in History Generates Optimism in the Midwest

by Bill Roberts

Aug. 20—In America's Midwest, in blue-collar counties where Donald Trump won big, the LaRouche Political Movement is on the ground organizing to defeat the British-backed coup against the Presidency. We are outside post offices and shopping centers with big signs that say, "Russiagate is a Fraud: Defend Trump." We are educating people on the harmony of interests inherent in reviving the American Credit System of Hamilton, Lincoln, and LaRouche, and on how we can achieve peace through economic development by working with China, Russia, and India.

In many counties of Ohio, West Virginia and upstate New York, the vote swing was as much as 10%-15% from previous Presidential elections, where support for establishment Republicans Mitt Romney and John McCain was lackluster, but voters resonated with Trump's commitment to rebuild the industrial economy and exit from bad free-trade deals and regime-change wars. While the media are trying to create an image of Trump as an isolated President whom only people on the extreme fringe still support, the reality on the ground is completely the opposite.

The pattern of responses to our initiative indicates a politically independent movement of LaRouche Democrats in strong support of President Trump—not simply on the basis of single issues, but in recognition that Donald Trump is kicking against the same pricks that ran a witch-hunt against Lyndon LaRouche 25 years ago. The American population was not politically mobilized to win the fight at that time.

Typical of the individuals signing up to join us, are workers in their thirties and forties who have never voted for anyone but a Democrat, until they voted for Donald Trump. Most are members of labor unions, and some are part of what remains of a highly skilled workforce tied to manufacturing. In Youngstown, Ohio, outside of a rally Trump addressed last month, scores of people identified themselves as LaRouche supporters—people who personally campaigned for Lyndon LaRouche during his many Presidential campaigns or

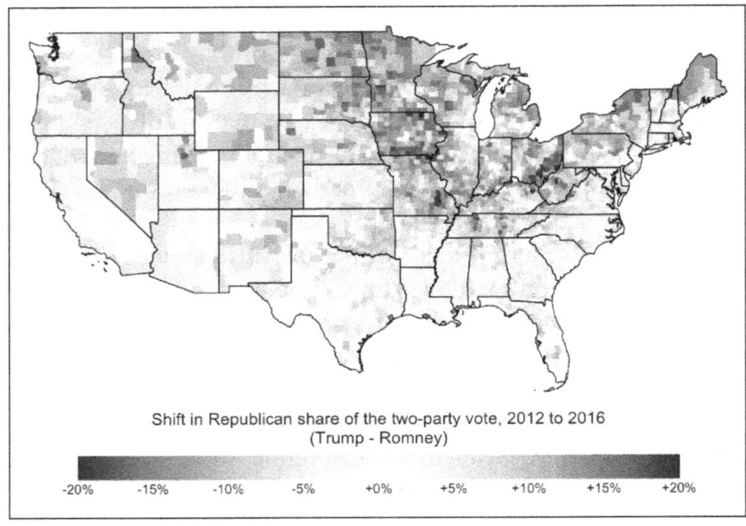

knew someone who had.

We are also meeting many veterans who want an end to the endless destabilizing wars, and people who were not political until the destruction known as the Obama Presidency. Many people respond by telling us how important it is that we are out there representing a voice for truth against this torrent of lies and hate.

Voters in these areas are not merely abandoning the Democratic Party in droves to defend Trump. Seeing all but five members of Congress voting to impose sanctions against Russia, and buying wholly into the now-disproven Russiagate fraud, confirmed in the minds of many that the President is really not a Republican—he is at war with the establishment in both parties. In other words, the sanctions bill was the point at which Trump's base was liberated from the Republican Party establishment, which never supported him. In states like Michigan, activists reported that the state Republican Party did virtually nothing to elect their Presidential nominee, or to protect the integrity of the voting process, leaving the campaigning up to parallel grass-roots organizations coordinating directly with the national Trump campaign.

In discussion with LaRouche PAC this past week, the head of a pro-Trump activist group in another Midwestern state indicated that his activist base was mainly made up of Democrats—members of labor unions and retired teachers. He was frustrated—sick of being called a racist and thrilled to hear of a plan to defeat the coup. He reported that in a town where the coal-mining operation went under and has been restarted since Trump's inauguration, six out of eight of the businesses that shut down have reopened, bringing back 300 jobs. The issue is the economy.

What is almost universally understood among this working-class layer in the Rust Belt, is that there is no compatibility between the "boom-bust" Wall Street monetarist system of theft, and the commitment to revolutionary advances in the productive capability of the nation—the American System—of which China is now the leading example. Reviving the American System has been the life's work and mission of Lyndon LaRouche, which made him the target of an operation much like the one targeting Trump today, to kill him or remove him from power.

In 2006, during a period of accelerated auto-plant shutdowns, Lyndon LaRouche initiated a campaign to reverse the devastation to the machine-tool sector of our economy, calling on Congress to draft an *Economic Recovery Act* for retooling idled auto manufacturing plants for the purpose of building critical national infrastructure. The automobile industry was really a "build anything" industry and could easily be repurposed under the direction of a new Federal corporation, to build components for high speed electrified rail, nuclear power plants, and the large lock gates found along our navigable waterways and rivers.

This proposal received extensive support from hundreds of state legislators, city and county governments, and many trade union locals and councils in the region, but it was defeated by the influence over Congress of investment banks and hedge funds, which proceeded to asset-strip much of the auto sector plant and equipment.

While the failed monetarist axioms of the top income strata of U.S. society have devastated the flyover regions where Donald Trump successfully campaigned for President, the ideas of Lyndon and Helga LaRouche have taken hold in Asia, where during the same period the Chinese government successfully curbed financial speculation and instituted a Hamiltonian system of banking, making a staggering volume of investment in public projects for the common benefit of the Chinese people and all the partner nations involved. The reality of that global shift, and President Trump's openness to work with China on the Belt and Road Initiative, is the basis

EIRNS

LPAC organzxing to support Trump in the Midwest.

upon which to move now for total victory against the dying British-empire directed trans-Atlantic system.

The desire for an economy not measured by monetary value, but by a harmonically combined future effect for mankind, as seen in China's Belt and Road Initiative, is the typical desire of the skilled American industrial worker.

Other forms of short-term survival, whether criminal, quasi-criminal or otherwise, fall under the category of "gettin' paid." From the standpoint of an increasingly productive industrial economy where people have good jobs (as President Trump correctly stated last week), it is not difficult to foresee an increasingly unified nation capable of solving any lingering problems.

As citizens realize the power of fighting alongside an international movement for peace and development, to finally destroy the British empire—which they are actually doing if they are effectively defending the Presidency—they are becoming very, very optimistic. The issue is not whether you root for Donald Trump, or think he is a great guy. The issue is whether you personally have the courage to take on the pricks who have been destroying this country and promoting war—in the way that Lyndon LaRouche has taken them on for the majority of his life. In a recent discussion with associates, in response to the renewed notoriety of LaRouche's role in U.S. politics, he responded, "It's not just me. It's not just me as a person. It's what I represent as an axis to strike for what needs to be struck. And that's the only thing I ever really did that was important."

BOOK REVIEW

Rogue Spooks

by Barbara Boyd

Rogue Spooks, The Intelligence War on Donald Trump
by Dick Morris and Eileen McGann
New York: St. Martin's Press, 2017
272 pages, hardcover, $27.99

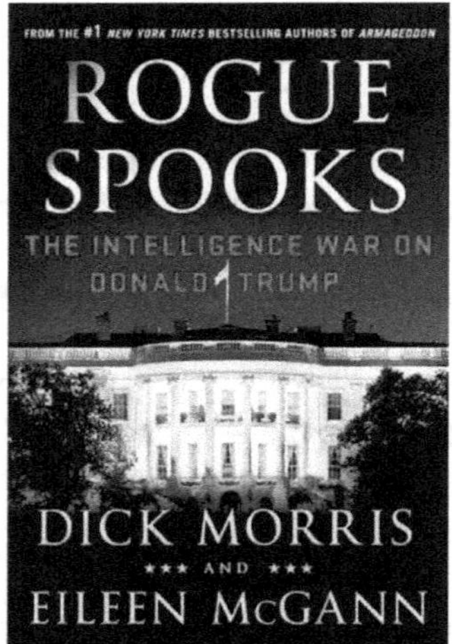

Aug. 17—Dick Morris and his wife Ellen McGann have written a new book, *Rogue Spooks, the Intelligence War on Trump.* It is to be commended for its dramatic and detailed account of the British government's wholesale interference in the 2016 U.S. Presidential election in favor of Hillary Clinton. Other than *EIR*, no other publication has so thoroughly focused on the British genesis of the coup against Trump.

Where Morris goes astray is in his assignment of the reasons why the British, and Obama's spooks working with them, are engaging in a coup to assassinate or neuter Trump. With one significant exception, he provides a gripping account of "who done it," with respect to the coup. He is wrong about their motive. To win the war presently facing the nation, the President and the American public must understand both aspects of the crime.

Morris was, of course, the famous pollster and advisor to Arkansas Governor and then President Bill Clinton. He got caught in a sexual scandal shortly before the Democratic Party convention nominated Clinton for a second term. Since that time he has become a controversial Republican populist with a wide national audience, and now his book is heading toward bestseller status. He was an early supporter of Donald Trump.

In the first four chapters, Morris shows how the dodgy British MI6 dossier, compiled by former MI6 agent Christopher Steele and Sir Andrew Wood, one of the highest ranking agents in the Queen's Service, was used to start the FBI investigation of Trump in the Summer of 2016, conducted by former showboat FBI Director James Comey. According to widespread British reporting, both Steele and Britain's Government Communications Headquarters (GCHQ) surveillance agency, were tasked to produce dirt on

CC/Andrew Dallos

Candidate Hillary Clinton (center) and Rachel Maddow (left) at MSNBC's Town Hall in Philadelphia, April 16, 2016.

James Comey (left), President Obama (center) and outgoing FBI Director Robert Mueller (right) at the June 21, 2013 announcement that Comey had been nominated to become FBI Director.

Trump, or those associated with him, which could be used to paint Trump as a Putin stooge. Morris demonstrates that the entire dossier was fake, and that the FBI, the Clinton campaign, and the British had to know it was fake. Morris gives all the details showing how Clinton repeatedly used the phony allegations against Trump in her campaign, and how this attack on Trump actually helped Clinton's candidacy.

After the election, the FBI under Comey wanted to pay Christopher Steele $50,000 to corroborate the phony dossier, and the FBI continued to collaborate with him through the efforts of Senator John McCain, former CIA director John Brennan, and James Comey. Just after President Trump's inauguration, Comey, and Obama's intelligence chiefs, went to Trump and presented him with the fake and salacious British dossier, in a fashion guaranteed to ensure its publication by the national news media. Morris correctly describes this episode as the closest thing there can be to a political assassination without a gun.

Morris acknowledges that the British account of the alleged Russian hack of the Democratic National Committee throws that aspect of the story into the question-mark category. According to that account, the Brits notified the FBI and the Democratic Party that the Russians had hacked the DNC in 2015, but the Democrats did absolutely nothing about it. The Democratic National Committee never allowed the FBI to forensically examine the allegedly hacked computers. The British account states that GCHQ and other elements of British intelligence had become concerned about meetings between Trump associates and the Russians, and Trump's "soft line" on Russia, as early as 2015.

This aspect of the British account, however, is designed to make it appear credible that the DNC computers were hacked by the Russians in a normal act of cyber-espionage. What happens to this story if there was no Russian hack—as demonstrated by the recent report of the Veterans Intelligence Professionals for Sanity? What happens if, as the VIPS allege, the DNC emails went to Wikileaks, where they were published—as the result of leaks by DNC insiders, not Russian hacks? What happens to this story line if the alleged GCHQ surveillance of "Trump associates" in conversation with the Russians does not exist, but was actually another faked report, to provide the basis for unparalleled intelligence community surveillance and attempts to entrap Presidential candidate Trump even before election day?

Otherwise, Morris presents an interesting account of Obama's deliberate efforts against Trump:

• Obama sabotaged Trump's ability to hire permanent staff by exhausting the budget of the National Se-

Retired U.S. Army Lieutenant General Michael Flynn at an October 2016 campaign rally for Donald Trump in Phoenix, Arizona.

A small sample of the relentless mass media assault on President Trump.

curity Council and other agencies.

• Obama's encouragement of his own civil service hires to stay in place to wage war against Trump from within the government.

• The political assassination of Michael Flynn by Democrats and establishment Republicans.

Morris also cites James Comey's efforts to set the President up, leading to the appointment of intended Grand Inquisitor Robert Mueller to finish the job.

He accounts for the great number of illegal classified leaks which have damaged the Presidency, by stating that John Brennan and Eric Holder purged the CIA and FBI of conservatives and put liberals firmly in place in these agencies.

He is very clear that the only way that the American people can defeat this coup, is to mobilize to prevent their Congressmen and Senators from entertaining the orchestrated media and "spook" lies intended to destroy President Trump.

To this end, Morris reminds us that the British deployed a candidate directly against Franklin Delano Roosevelt, in the form of Wendell Willkie. He also traces the incredible number of cases of U.S.-staged coups and assassinations in other countries to change undesired election results. He claims that he and Bill Clinton intervened directly to elect Boris Yeltsin to a second term in Russia, by providing polling services and political direction to Yeltsin's campaign from President Clinton himself.

Where Morris falls short, is in his cramped and very partisan view of why all of this is happening. He claims that the British wanted to get Obama to act against the Russians, because Obama was soft on arming Ukrainians in that ongoing conflict on Russia's border. He fails to understand that Obama was a British plant from the get-go, who always acted on the basis of ultimate British grand strategy.

He provides some history of the FBI, CIA and other intelligence agencies, implying that they act primarily in their bureaucratic self-interest. But he also fails to understand that these agencies have been virtual British satrapies ever since Franklin Roosevelt died.

Ultimately, he fails to figure out that the ultimate British weapon is control of the American mind—control of the axioms by which we think. Free trade, for example, was an economic model against which we fought a revolution. As a result, our Constitution specifies that federal credit for productive purposes and the power to issue money, are under the control of the Federal government, not the monetarists on Wall Street. Unfortunately, this is not the political truth by which Morris, the author of the famous pragmatic Clinton strategy of "triangulation," lives.

The immediate motive for the coup against President Trump, is the Belt and Road Initiative (BRI), in which Russia and China have joined to develop the world. Trump has signaled a willingness to work with both Xi Jinping and Vladimir Putin on this great project of physical economic development of the entire planet. Were he to do this—bringing millions of productive jobs to the United States—the British imperial model of control of the world would be consigned to the dustbin of history. That is the reason why the British are out to kill, impeach, or otherwise incapacitate this President.

British 'State Capture' of South Africa Must End!

by David Cherry and Ramasimong Phillip Tsokolibane

Aug. 19—South African President Jacob Zuma, facing a many-sided regime-change scheme, narrowly survived a parliamentary vote of no confidence by secret ballot on Aug. 8, in which at least twenty-six MPs of his own party, the African National Congress (ANC), voted against him. This was not merely a constitutionally recognized procedure; it was part of a larger, British directed regime-change mobilization.

Americans and South Africans may not realize that they suffer from the same problem—British neocolonialism—including, at this moment, parallel attempts at regime change. The propaganda war to overthrow President Trump is at full tilt, including public incitements to his assassination. (See Barbara Boyd's review of *Rogue Spooks: The Intelligence War on Donald Trump*, by Dick Morris and Eileen McGann, in this issue.)

But it is not just the fate of two nations that is at issue. Both America and South Africa are crucial in the larger strategic struggle that will determine the fate of the world—whether it will collapse in economic failure and world war, or whether a new paradigm will take hold to bring humanity to a higher level of material, moral, and cognitive existence than it has yet known.

For South Africa to pull its weight toward that goal, it must reverse its current de-industrialization and accelerate in the opposite direction. Concretely: Will President Zuma and his faction succeed in their turn to the East, to adopt some approximation of Hamiltonian economics, as China has done, or will the British Empire prevail, ensuring the continuation of the ongoing, twenty-year de-industrialization of South Africa?

Tension was high in South Africa on the day of the vote, and security measures in and around Parliament were in place, while the ANC and the opposition each had many thousands at rallies near Parliament in Cape Town, and around the country.

If eleven more MPs had voted against Zuma, providing a simple majority for the no confidence motion (given some absences and abstentions), he and his cabinet would have had to resign. In a National Assembly of 400 seats, the ANC has 249. The opposition was jubilant for having come so close.

This was the eighth vote of no confidence against

Kopano Tlape/GCIS

The South African National Assembly, the lower house of Parliament, Feb. 16, 2017.

President Xi Jinping of China and South African President Jacob Zuma shake hands at BRICS summit in Brazil, 2014.

Zuma in one form or another since 2010, when Zuma's government got serious about joining what was then just the BRIC. The larger, ongoing process is one in which the two main opposition parties (both British-owned) and the mass media carry out total propaganda warfare to vilify Zuma and his ANC faction, punctuated by these no confidence votes to demonstrate and reinforce their progress toward toppling the government. Both sides are looking toward the national elections in December 2019, with the longer term success or failure of the Zuma faction in the balance.

In the debate preceding the vote of no confidence, the ANC took a turn in the right direction. Its MPs acknowledged the process just described for what it is. They accused the opposition of using the combination of mass media warfare and the no confidence vote to achieve what they had not achieved at the ballot box, as seen in these condensed extracts:

Minister of Arts and Culture Nathi Mthethwa: "A ramification of the unipolar world order is the demand for regime change across the globe ... to remove those who refuse to kow-tow to an oppressive global hegemony. Similarly, the call for regime change in South Africa today is to destabilize and subvert our democratic order. A major fallacy raised by the opposition is that the recession was caused by the cabinet reshuffle [notably, the firing of Finance Minister and London darling, Pravin Gordhan]. The threat of the recession developed in the preceding two quarters. The first S&P downgrade to sub-investment level was decided before the cabinet reshuffle. It is disingenuous to suggest that the recession was caused by the reshuffle. Thus this motion is based on fake news. The target of this motion is the authority of government; they aim for a coup d'etat to overthrow a legitimate government through destabilization." Mthethwa is a former minister of police.

Deputy Chief Whip Doris Dlakude: "This insurrectionist opposition ... has a publicly stated intention of regime change, to manipulate the legislature and the constitution to collapse government and sow the seeds of chaos in society to ultimately grab power."

Defense Minister Nosisiwe Mapisa-Nqakula and Pule Mabe of the ANC National Executive Committee followed, also using the language of an attempted coup d'etat.

The opposition went crazy, interrupting again and again with purported points of order. (Deputy Speaker of the House: "That is not a point of order, and screaming will not make it so.") The debate was carried live on national TV and the Internet.

Zuma—who now has a Finance Minister sympathetic to the spirit of the BRICS, Malusi Gigaba—followed up his victory in the no confidence vote by officially launching the Africa Regional Center of the BRICS' New Development Bank (NDB) in Johannesburg on Aug. 17.

At that event, Zuma emphasized to the NDB President, K.V. Kamath, members of the diplomatic corps,

South African Finance Minister Malusi Gigaba.

cabinet ministers, and leaders of industry and finance, that setting up the Africa Regional Center shows the bank is working to expand its membership to other countries beyond the five BRICS members, saying, "We certainly trust that African countries will be among the first to take up membership at the New Development Bank. … The biggest challenge is that Africa remains largely unindustrialized, with the result that our economies are overexposed to the whims of commodities markets."

NDB President Kamath announced that the bank would like to fund $1.5 billion of projects in South Africa over the next 18 months.

I. The Mighty Wurlitzer

Only days before the no confidence vote, LaRouche South Africa had circulated to MPs and many others, a paper on the same wavelength as the ANC speakers quoted above, stating:

The British-guided, multifarious opposition to the ruling Zuma faction and the ANC more generally—consisting of political parties, NGOs, academic institutes, commentators, and the press—is like the Mighty Wurlitzer, a theatre organ of the days before World War II. It can dominate the airwaves, and the brainwaves, with any melody of its master's choice. The likeness to the Mighty Wurlitzer was first used by the CIA's first chief of political warfare, Frank Wisner, to describe his worldwide propaganda machine. And it is also what the Presidency of Donald Trump is facing in the United States at this moment.

The British and their agents are pulling out all the stops of their Mighty Wurlitzer to push South Africans' buttons with every conceivable half-truth, lie, and fantasy against the Zuma government and the ANC. Thus, every so often, one of the opposition parties calls for a vote of no confidence as a kind of battering ram, attempting to keep Zuma and the government off balance and diverted from the tasks of government, and with the ultimate goal of toppling him, and splintering his faction and the ANC at large. This is not constitutional democracy; it is regime change. Britain's new High Commissioner to South Africa, Nigel Casey—having come straight from 10 Downing Street as an advisor to the prime minister, and with regime change experience—presides over this hideous performance of the music of Hell.

This is happening because South Africa is important on the world stage, and is a serious threat to the British neocolonial empire.

What Is at Stake

Think of South Africa in relation to the single most important process on foot in the world today—the rise of China as a productive economy and China's decision to export its success—through the now famous Belt and Road Initiative—to countries who wish for such success themselves. China is offering infrastructure and manufacturing capacity in exchange for whatever an African, Asian, or other country—even potentially the United States—has to offer. In China, *manufacturing as a percentage of gross domestic product (GDP)* is an astounding forty percent. In Sub-Saharan Africa, in which South Africa is the leader, South Africa's percentage is now only thirteen percent.[1] For China's initiative to succeed, it needs the cooperation of its partner, South Africa, which has the only full-set economy on the continent and the highest literacy rate, 94%. South Africa is the gateway for the industrialization of Africa!

Opposing China's initiative is the British Empire, including the U.S. Establishment of the Bushes and Obama. The British will not stand idly by, while its economic model for Africa—once accurately described by the late John Garang of Sudan as "misery management"—is crushed by the bulldozers, caterpillar tractors, rail lines, and steel mills of the new Africa. The Empire believes it can prevent the Chinese initiative—and the closely related BRICS process—from bursting out beyond the Eurasian continent. And perhaps—the British oligarchs believe—the entire Belt and Road initiative can be rolled up.

In August 2016 the oligarchs succeeded in toppling Brazilian President Dilma Rousseff—who brought her country into the BRICS—in a regime-change process similar to the one now underway in South Africa. They overthrew Argentine President Cristina Fernández de Kirchner, another enthusiast for the BRICS process, in December 2015, after a campaign of lies and vilification. Both presidents were succeeded by political allies of the vulture capitalists who are now dismantling the state sector in the two countries.

What is at stake, therefore, is not just the success of

---

1. South Africa's leadership in industrialization is clearly seen in the size of its workforce in manufacturing, construction, and electricity/water/gas, as a percentage of its total population—5.8% in 2014, compared to Kenya, 1.0%; and Nigeria, less than 1.0%.

Xinhua

President Jacob Zuma's political machine is the only formation in South Africa that the British empire fears. Zuma is prepared to take the country back from the empire.

President Zuma's political machine is the only formation in South Africa that the British empire fears. It is the only one that has the guts to say, as Zuma himself recently told Mmusi Maimane, the leader of the opposition in Parliament, "Don't feed me your English words from London!" The Zuma machine is at present the only one that is actually prepared to take the country back from the empire and adopt an economic model for the development of the country that will actually work.

The proper name for that model is the system of Public Credit, as designed by the American founding father, Alexander Hamilton. Hamilton's approach is best represented today in the economic initiatives of the People's Republic of China. Even China's detractors will tell you that in China, in the past thirty years, 700 million people have risen up out of the direst poverty. And that, above all else in the world, is what the British empire fears.

The British know that they can no longer prevail in South Africa. A government that continues to depend on the economics of London and Wall Street, will bring unending strife. The British objective at this point is not to prevail, but to ensure that the forces represented by the Zuma faction also do not prevail. Strife and chaos are, therefore, the British preference, whatever the government. They will sacrifice their own friends in South Africa, when necessary, to achieve it.

the Belt and Road Initiative in Africa. It is a question of whether the British empire—by stopping the initiative in South America and Africa—might be able to go so far as to actually strangle the child in its cradle, so that the evil of the British empire may survive. South Africans must see their responsibility to the human race in this light. The world needs the help of South Africa.

State Capture

Britain has owned South Africa for the past two hundred years, since the time of the Napoleonic wars. It has ruled South Africa for the benefit of its empire, first with boots on the ground, and now as a neocolonial empire held together by financial, propaganda, and psychological warfare. Today, President Zuma and his ruling faction of the ANC are challenging British hegemony, and they can and must win: There is no other issue. Corruption is not the issue. The wrongdoing of the Gupta brothers is not the issue. These are very serious problems, but they are being used as surrogates.

The British—having failed to achieve regime change after three years of trying—have finally opted to crown their accusations with the supreme charge, that Jacob Zuma is attempting to "capture the state." With that lie, they are taking a great risk. It could prompt many South Africans to realize that Zuma is attempting to rescue the state from British state capture. "But he is not proceeding in a democratic manner!" the gremlins howl. There is indeed another level of democracy, which functions outside of *Robert's Rules of Order*.

Strategy for Victory

The required strategy—under the current condition of sharpened battle—has at least the following features. The South African people must be mobilized on the basis of a vision for a better future. They must know that *there is a better future*, and they must be made aware of what that future entails. Using surrogate issues in this battle will fail. Such issues have no potential to call forth a fighting people. There must be a bold turning away from the British trans-Atlantic empire and towards the BRICS and the East. This must be done by asserting leadership in the credit-directed development of Africa, and the building up of South Africa's capabilities for that purpose.

South Africans must be told that the enemy is the

The signing of the agreement for the launch of the African Regional Center of the New Development Bank (the BRICS bank) in Johannesburg, Aug. 17. From left: the bank's President K.V. Kamath, Zuma, Gigaba, and South African Minister of International Relations Maite Nkoana-Mashabane.

South Africa's Imperial Origins

During the long period of white rule, the British Empire attempted to crush the independence of the Dutch and Huguenot-descended Afrikaner people (largely *boere*, farmers) and their institutions, and also destroy and pulverize the Black African kingdoms. The Afrikaners, many of whom had abandoned the Cape Colony to form two republics of their own—the South African Republic and the Orange Free State, north and south of the River Vaal, respectively— were the harder nut to crack of the two, being better armed and more easily unified than the African kingdoms.

The British empire provoked the Second Anglo-Boer War, 1899-1902, when it became clear that the South African Republic under President Paul Kruger might succeed in building a railway to the port of Beira on the Indian Ocean. Such a railway was a projection of power that the British saw as a threat.

The British vastly underestimated the Afrikaners' potential for resistance. The commander of the British forces, Field Marshal Frederick Roberts, 1st Earl Roberts, VC, KG, KP, GCB, OM, GCSI, GCIE, KStJ, VD, PC, and after him, Lord Kitchener, were only able to defeat Afrikaner guerrilla operations with a scorched earth policy. Afrikaner farms were burned to the ground and more than 100,000 Afrikaners—largely women and children—were thrown into concentration camps, where, at a minimum, 27,000 died of disease and starvation. (It is less well known that the British also put Blacks in concentration camps during the war, in which at least 13,000 died, and possibly very many more.[2])

British neocolonial empire. They must also understand that British subjects, and South African citizens of British heritage, are not *ipso facto* representatives of the empire. They are largely victims of the empire, like everyone else.

And because there are many weaknesses and failures in the current government, actions are needed to demonstrate immediately the government's resolve to break through to solutions of at least some of these problems, as the initial steps of an ongoing process of renewal. A defensive posture with respect to such problems will guarantee defeat.

For South Africans, and others, to get a proper perspective on the present moment and break out of the controlled environment of the Mighty Wurlitzer, it is necessary to discover the history of the highly political struggle for South Africa's industrialization, little known today.

II. Industrialize or Die!

South Africa presents a case in which the current leadership and government, under majority rule, are the heirs of a long period of rule by Brit and Boer, at the expense of Black Africans. We do not have the power to choose our forerunners, but we may be capable of learning from them.

---

2. Stowell Kessler, *The Black Concentration Camps of the Anglo-Boer War, 1899-1902*, Bloemfontein: War Museum of the Boer Republics, 2012. While deserving of longer treatment, the imposition of apartheid on South Africa was supported by the same British oligarchs against whom the Anglo-Boer Wars were fought. The British racists realized that this policy was a factor inhibiting South African economic development by barbarously limiting the creative powers of the black work force. But the Afrikaner drive for industrialization—which the British failed to stop—eventually created a paradoxical condition which, under visionary leadership, would force a choice between economic collapse

Through this savagery the British had, in a very important sense, lost the war. Lord Alfred Milner, his successor Lord Selborne, and the Milner Kindergarten were indeed able form the Union of South Africa as a single country under British imperial rule, through the successful negotiation of the Constitution of 1910—bringing together the Cape Colony, Natal, and the two Afrikaner republics. But the Afrikaners and their institutions had not been crushed, and the British were obliged to mollify their smoldering hatred by allowing them a major role in political life.

Black Africans also had their rage. Some had fought on one side and some on the other. They saw that the constitutional settlement of 1910 was the coming together of the whites to exclude them from power. During the war, some British had hinted, and some had promised, that in exchange for support or neutrality, Africans would be rewarded with political rights. It never happened. For the whites, the interests of the blacks did not weigh in the balance.

Jan Smuts, Prime Minister of South Africa, 1919-1924 and 1939-1948.

Industry vs. Empire

Industrialization and protection for infant industries became burning issues for Afrikaners after World War I. It was then that the prices of primary products worldwide slid ever downward for a decade, but South Africa had to live by its export of primary products. The National Party, led by Barry Hertzog, saw the answer in industrialization.

But Hertzog and his party were not in power. Jan Smuts of the South African Party was prime minister from 1919-1924, and Smuts, although an Afrikaner, loved the British, and for the British he was a godsend who could reconcile a large number of Afrikaners to British policy. Smuts took what he thought were expe-

dient steps to give his government the appearance of supporting industrialization.

In 1919, he prevailed upon the physicist, Hendrik Johannes van der Bijl (pronounced *fun da bayle*) to return to South Africa from the United States and to establish institutions for scientific research. Van der Bijl was a genius who had taken his doctorate in physics at the University of Leipzig. At the Royal School of Technology in Dresden, he had continued his research, which led to the thermionic vacuum tube that made wireless telephony and telegraphy possible. But van der Bijl was more than a brilliant scientist. In the United States, he had been one of nineteen scientists who had associated themselves as the Society of Planners and Builders.

Van der Bijl's own agenda called for using the powers of government to greatly increase the production of electricity through a state-owned enterprise, the Electricity Supply Commission (Eskom); to establish another state-owned company to produce iron and steel (Iscor); and to develop the country's rail network. Smuts endorsed van der Bijl's plan for Eskom, which was established by law in 1922, and allowed him to investigate and make recommendations for iron and steel production. Unwittingly, Smuts had played a crucial role in initiating industrialization. He had done what he thought was politically expedient, but he was not wholeheartedly in support of van der Bijl's plans.

Smuts leaned toward a British free trade policy. It came out in the election campaign of 1924. His biographer, Keith Hancock, writes,

"In his election manifesto, Smuts assured the country that he stood for a bold industrial policy; but he did not give the same bold assurance of tariff protection for South African industries. Whereas Hertzog and [the Labour Party's Frederic] Creswell promised Protection with a capital P, the most that Smuts promised was 'discriminating protection for those industries especially suited to the country.'"

Hertzog won the election and formed a National-Labour cabinet. The Hertzog government was strongly

---

and an end to apartheid. South Africa found that visionary leadership in Nelson Mandela and his Afrikaner partner, F.W. de Klerk, in creating the modern South Africa that the British are still attempting to destroy. This history shows how true policies of Hamiltonian development create paradoxes that can force people to bridge what are thought to be intractable and unbridgeable differences.

oriented to the projects of van der Bijl's agenda. That did not mean, however, that these projects had smooth sailing. Apart from the obstacles often created by rocky economic conditions, the British free trade ideology—so thoroughly developed by Adam Smith in his attack on the American Revolution of 1776—was everywhere.

The plan for protection of infant industries naturally angered the British. Hertzog appointed a close collaborator of van der Bijl, Andries Johannes Bruwer, as Chairman of the Board of Trade and Industries in 1924. Bruwer drew up what he has called, "South Africa's Industrial Magna Carta" for protection. Hertzog's British-influenced finance minister rejected it. But an emergency cabinet meeting then approved Bruwer's work, and he was asked to draft the necessary legislation. Bruwer later wrote, "This was a memorable day for South Africa, a day when its rulers became practically aware of its colossal industrial potential."[3]

Eskom was also targeted. Van der Bijl had planned Eskom as a government controlled corporation, insofar as the government appointed the members of the board and could replace them, and it appointed its auditors. It was to plow its earnings back into the corporation to pursue the goal of cheap and abundant energy for the country. Otherwise, Eskom was to operate as a private

Alice Jacobs, *South African Heritage*

H.J. van der Bijl
(1887-1948)

company would. It would have no monopoly.

According to Alice Jacobs, van der Bijl's biographer, writing in 1948, the Eskom plan "raised storms of criticism and opposition. ... How the skeptical onlookers smirked... 'How,' they asked, 'could any undertaking deprived of the profit-making incentive of all business, be run efficiently?' However, it did work—so well that it is now held up as an example of how public utility companies should be run."

In 1932, after ten years, van der Bijl saw a need to raise capital for extensions to Eskom's operations, and to repay a loan of £8 million from the government Treasury at the "high" rate of interest of 5%, with which Eskom had begun. "He decided not to follow the usual precedent of floating all large loans overseas, but to try to raise the money in South Africa." A loan of £500,000 was immediately oversubscribed. The next year, he sought £2,500,000; again it was oversubscribed. The next funding, in 1934, was for £6,750,000 (Jacobs describes it as a loan in one place, but as a stock issue in another). "The banks refused to underwrite the whole amount," but "within forty hours the whole ... was fully subscribed."

After fourteen years of operation, Eskom had cut the average price of electricity in half.

Iron and Steel

The Iron and Steel Industrial Corporation (Iscor) was created by law in 1928, and as with Eskom, van der Bijl was named chairman. The new creation unleashed the fury of the British-steered press. Smuts objected that Iscor would compete with private enterprise, that is, with companies in Britain, since private iron and steel producing enterprises in South Africa were small affairs. But the issue of competition was a diversion. Smuts was responding to British direction coming from a higher level than British business: Steel means power, the power to produce one's own turbines, rails, and railroad cars. At this very time—the late 1920s—H.G. Wells, the British empire toady, wrote that there was

---

3. Bruwer's earlier doctoral dissertation at Harvard, *Protection in South Africa*, had been rejected because he insisted on including a chapter on "South Africa and Imperial Preference" that was highly unflattering to the Empire. In it, he refers to Prof. W.J. Ashley as British Prime Minister Joseph Chamberlain's "right-hand man" and quotes from Ashley's *The Tariff Problem* (1903), Chapter 5: "It will be necessary to get a gradually increasing amount of the Colonial trade away from other nations, or the Colonies will drift further and further away from Great Britain and become economically independent." Bruwer's chapter ends with this parting shot: "Would that the labor of economists since the advent of Adam Smith were not in vain, and that the 'enlightened' twentieth century has something better in store for the world than a revival of mercantilism." A.J. Bruwer, *Protection in South Africa* (Stellenbosch: Pro Ecclesia, 1923), pp. 148, 170. Upon rejection, Bruwer packed up and went to the University of Pennsylvania, where his dissertation was approved.

entirely too much steel being produced in the world, as part of his rant against industrialization.

One of the arguments against a steel industry in South Africa was that there was no market for it. That is exactly what is said today against building additional nuclear power plants—that, according to expert projections, the energy will not be needed for thirty years or more. Similarly it is argued today that there is not enough demand to justify building a steel mill in Limpopo province, just when all Africa is gaining a new optimism that a continental network of railroads can be built, and many new dams and hydroelectric plants.

The enemies of rising living standards for the mass of humanity, know very well that it is precisely the steel mill, the power plant, and the railroad that *stimulate* productive activity. Use the steel to build a transcontinental railroad, and new cities will spring up along the way. Provide cheap and abundant electricity, and new efficiencies emerge to free the worker and the business

---

Van der Bijl on Industrialization

These quotations, illustrating the tendency of H.J. van der Bijl's thought, are from Alice Jacobs' *South African Heritage: A Biography of H.J. van der Bijl.*

"In matters of science and engineering, as in music, which is the only language of all nations— we move in a sphere far above that which teaches us to recognize lines of demarcation between different members of the great human family."

—At the First World Power Conference (electric power) in London in 1924

"This [the city of Vanderbijlpark] must not be just an Iscor preserve; it must be an industrial city providing avenues of employment as the gold mines dwindle. That is the only solution to the poverty of the majority of our people—it is the only sure way of raising the standard of living for all—black and white." He called it his "city of ideas and ideals."

—Jacobs reports that van der Bijl often said this in 1947-1948

---

enterprise to address new challenges, to perform higher tasks.

When a new campaign against Iscor was launched in 1935, just a year after Iscor was fully up and running, van der Bijl hit back in an address to the Association of Certificated Mechanical and Electrical Engineers, in October:

I wish to refer particularly to the recent frantic outburst of criticism in part of our press against Iscor, against me and against our Government. I say part of our press, because not all the newspapers associate themselves with the rubbish that has recently been published about this great undertaking. . . .

When one reads some of the criticisms . . . one is led to believe that the people of South Africa are against the undertaking to establish an iron and steel industry, and the man in the street is led to believe that the undertaking has turned out a fiasco. . . . Every department is producing considerably in excess of the guaranteed capacity of the plant. We are selling all the steel we can make, and since last July we have been making substantial profits. . . . Several important subsidiary industries have been established as a direct result of the advent of Iscor—and this is only a beginning. . . . In the face of all this, one must still breathe this discouraging atmosphere. . .

But the hostile campaign continued. Academic economists "assailed the 'hopelessly uneconomic' performance of Iscor in its early years." Yet, in 1940, Iscor produced 320,000 tons of steel and met about one-third of the country's requirements; by 1950, this had increased to over 600,000 tons, almost half of the steel used in South Africa.

Whatever the wishes of the British empire, a prodigious number of South Africans of British heritage worked to make Eskom, Iscor, and related enterprises a success.

World War II

Jan Smuts was returned to power just four days after Hitler invaded Poland on September 1, 1939. Smuts was now the head of the United Party, the then dominant, British-steered party that included most South Africans of British heritage and most of those Afrikaners who did not aggressively put Afrikaner nationalism first. He was willing to bring South Africa into the war on the side of the Allies, and was tasked by the British to quickly gear up the South African economy for war production. That economic system so feared and despised by the British in peace time was suddenly in favor, now that Britain was at war.

Smuts called upon van der Bijl to urgently organize the country's industrial production for war, making him Director-General of War Supplies. "His powers were enormous—far greater than those of a Cabinet Minister," according to G.R.D. Harding, the Eskom general manager. What van der Bijl accomplished during the war was a giant step forward in South Africa's industrialization, and he looked forward to maintaining this momentum after the war.

Van der Bijl and Smuts were not operating in a political vacuum. The larger picture was one of tension between British Prime Minister Winston Churchill and U.S. President Franklin Roosevelt, between the imperial idea and the hatred of empire. Each had a plan for the postwar world.

Roosevelt and South Africa

During the war, there were intense fights between Churchill and Roosevelt as to what would be the future postwar order. Roosevelt insisted that the United States was not fighting the war to protect the British, French, and Dutch empires, and that after the war, those empires must be dismantled. Churchill would become furious and insist that he had not been made Prime Minister to preside over the dissolution of the "Empah." These fights were reported by Elliott Roosevelt in his book about his father, *As He Saw It* (1946). As his father's *aide de camp*, he had been a witness.

Roosevelt recognized the importance of South Africa for his postwar vision of dismantling the empires. He corresponded with Smuts, and he was especially interested in the work of van der Bijl. In 1936, while in Washington for the world conference on electric power, van der Bijl was invited to make a presentation to Roosevelt. According to van der Bijl's biographer:

"At the time, he was not unduly impressed with the Roosevelt administration or the 'New Deal.' However, when he actually met the President, he felt to his amazement that he was in the presence of the most powerful personality he had ever encountered. He has never forgotten this experience, and FDR still stands out as quite the most impressive figure in the galaxy of famous people he has met."[4]

----

4. Alice Jacobs, *South African Heritage: A Biography of H.J. van der Bijl*, Pietermaritzburg, South Africa: Shuter & Shooter, 1948.

Years later, during the war, Roosevelt recommended to Smuts that van der Bijl be made chairman of the Joint Supply Council that Roosevelt wanted formed to decide what U.S. mining machinery was essential for South Africa to import during wartime, to keep the economy going.

Van der Bijl's speech during a tour of munitions factories in October 1940 was in step with Roosevelt's thinking. He spoke of the insight provided by the war experience, insight "into our great industrial potential—a potential which, if suitably guided, can be used as a powerful driving force in the period of economic reconstruction which must follow the war." He said that "South Africa can, with its own brains and materials, embark upon a new era of industrial development that will have a profound effect in increasing the affluence of our people and raising the standard of living of the poorer sections of the community."

Van der Bijl, like Roosevelt, was aware that this was not the outlook of the British Empire. In 1945, we find this sentence—with its scarcely concealed reference to the empire—in the middle of a discourse by van der Bijl on the importance of industrialization for peace and order in the world: "With each nation developing along the lines most suited to it *and with no nation endeavoring to prevent the peaceful industrial development of other nations*, the stable world economy emerging will, in my opinion, be the strongest factor in helping to ensure a peaceful and progressive world …" (emphasis added).

III. To Reverse Industrialization

During the war, Black workers were needed as never before—industry required the urbanization and participation of more and more of the Black population. There was a 72% increase in the numbers of Black workers in private manufacturing between 1939 and 1946, as 134,000 African workers entered industrial employment.

These workers sought better pay and better conditions, and there were strikes, especially when the end of the war was on the horizon. When the war ended in 1945, the workers' self-confidence and militance did not just evaporate. Many Blacks had served in the war far from home, and had gained greater self assurance and knowledge of the wider world. There were more strikes. Smuts would not yield on any matter of substance, and the strikes were put down. But it was clear that relations between black workers and white bosses in the postwar world would never be the same as before.

The British Empire was dead set against the continued industrialization of South Africa, which the empire itself had encouraged during the war. The British policy was that South Africa should scale back its industry.[5] But the wartime industrial build-up still had momentum and domestic political support after the war. There were also large settler communities in Kenya and Rhodesia (now Zimbabwe) that were potentially dangerous to the empire. These white settler communities, largely of British heritage, had political opposition elements of an anti-imperial nature, as in the case of the Afrikaners in South Africa, with thoughts of becoming independent, and they looked to South Africa for leadership. They, too, had industrialization on their minds.

Outeniqua George Railway Museum

The British royal family tours South Africa, 1947. At left, Jan Smuts and King George VI.

Posing as the Friend of the African

The British oligarchs had already decided that—to stop this industrialization impulse and maintain their imperial mastery—they would now pose as the friend of the Black African throughout Sub-Saharan Africa, against the European colonial settlers, even those of British descent. The decision to pose as "the friend of the African" was already evident, long before World War II, in London's response to a threatened coup by the colonial settlers in Kenya against the British governor in 1923, over racial policy, which the governor was attempting to soften only slightly. The Kenya White Paper of 1923 warned the settlers:

> Primarily Kenya is an African territory, and His Majesty's Government think it necessary definitely to record their considered opinion that the interests of the African natives must be para-

mount, and that if and when those interests and the interests of the immigrant races should conflict, the former should prevail.[6]

That was a statement of how the British government would play the game of empire in Africa, and dealing with South Africa would be the cornerstone. But the implementation of such a momentous change of appearances—from a colonial oppressor into "friend of the African"—was not like crossing the street. Each settler community would have to be dealt with according to its own circumstances.

Putting the National Party in Power

For South Africa, London's decision was to do the seemingly unthinkable—to throw the 1948 election to the National Party, the country's strongest party of Afrikaner nationalism. Let the Afrikaner nationalists face the rising anger and determination of the Blacks! Then "we British" can side with the Blacks to crush forever the independent power of Afrikaner nationalism and industrialism.

The evidence that the British threw the 1948 election to the National Party is clear enough, contrary to endless British propaganda.

Smuts and his United Party were the premier instruments of the British empire in South Africa, and South Africa was of strategic importance to the empire in

---

5. This policy was expressed, for example, in the publication of Lord Milner's group, *The Round Table Journal: A Quarterly Review of the Politics of the British Empire*, issue of December 1945.

6. Carroll Quigley, *Tragedy and Hope, A History of the World in Our Time*, 1966.

multiple ways. In 1947 the British royal family made its first-ever state visit to South Africa, which began when the royal family disembarked at Cape Town on Feb. 17, fifteen months before the election. They criss-crossed the country, visiting every city and many towns for almost ten weeks, with Smuts almost always at their side. It was implicitly a campaign tour for Smuts' United Party, and King George made every effort to make a show of friendship to the Afrikaners, which was what Smuts needed. But it was also an opportunity for the monarchy to gather intelligence and evaluate the state of the country.

After the departure of the royal visitors, Smuts began to show pessimism about the election for the first time, privately, to just two or three correspondents. He wrote, "All other governments have fallen in this post-war time—why should I not fall too?" In the ensuing months Smuts conducted a non-campaign. The inaction and lack of energy were apparent to his closest associates. He scarcely allowed his party to fight for victory, keeping it in a defensive position. Younger MPs and activists in the party could not understand it.

A key element in Smuts' sabotage of his own party was his refusal to make a justifiable change in the electoral law that many of the party's leaders believed would have guaranteed his victory. The Constitution of 1910—the deal between British and Afrikaners that locked Blacks out—gave a handicap to rural voters. Afrikaners were largely rural, and British settlers were largely urban. The roads were poor in 1910, and rural settlers were at a disadvantage in getting to the polls, so the law weighted rural votes to compensate. But by the end of the war, the network of roads was well developed. A change in the law was justified, and Smuts had a large enough majority in the House of Assembly to make the change.

Smuts did not significantly mobilize his party for the election until the last 30 days before election day, May 26, while the National Party was on a roll for 18 months. He had a weak network of volunteers and few professionals, while the National Party's organizers were on fire, using their noxious *swart gevaar* (black

@Eskom_SA

An Eskom Talent and Skills representative explains the selection criteria for Eskom bursaries at Amajuna District Career Symposium, KwaZulu-Natal, in August 2017.

threat) propaganda. In the election, if all votes had been counted without weighting, there would have been 80 seats in Parliament for Smuts, and 60 for D.F. Malan of the National Party, with 10 seats going to others who were largely pro-Smuts. But Smuts had lost.

The mighty Smuts—hero of the British empire, member of Churchill's War Cabinet, and an architect of the United Nations—had been discarded like a chewing gum wrapper.

Van der Bijl was a more serious threat. He was diagnosed with rectal cancer in 1948, but his doctors were apparently slow in deciding on the exploratory operation that led to the diagnosis. After the exploratory operation, they wrote that the cancer was inoperable. They didn't tell him that, but allowed him to believe he was recovering, thereby forestalling any initiative on his part for a second opinion. He died in December at the age of 61.

There are decades more to this story, including a setback for the empire when the momentum of van der Bijl's work led to South Africa's decision to build the first nuclear power plant on the African continent. There were further setbacks when Nelson Mandela twice forestalled a bloody race war that the empire would have found more than acceptable.

It was this industrialization process that, contrary to the intentions of its organizers, led to the liberation of Black South Africa. As industrialization proceeded, and more and more Africans were drawn into the large town-

The Koeberg nuclear power plant near Cape Town.

decolonization was also a question of prolonging the empire. Decolonization was never intended in economic and diplomatic terms. Cohen was the first to realize that an alliance with black nationalism was the key to *prolonging colonial rule.*"

Incredibly, London became the world headquarters of the struggle against apartheid, and South Africans in exile flocked to London. The British let the world know that *they* were the beneficent ones, even while they continued to exercise extensive remote control over the National Party government through control over the economy and the judiciary. They wanted to put Blacks in power from very un-African motives—from imperial motives—in the belief that Blacks would be more malleable, more easily controlled, than the white settlers, saying in effect, "Let them have political power. We will retain hegemony in the economic and propaganda spheres."

Yes, Black South Africans, the British empire was there to help you. When you or your parents—on your way into exile—crossed into Botswana at night, those nice chaps from MI6 were there to see you safely to town or to an encampment. They helped you—but with a different agenda. When Nelson Mandela was released in 1990 and it became possible to think of a negotiated transition, Her Majesty's High Commissioner, Sir Robin Renwick, had already reached out to you. He is now Lord Renwick, vice chairman of JP Morgan Cazenove, with multiple mining interests. But he reached out on behalf of imperial interests. The British say they have no permanent friends, only permanent interests. For once, the truth! The preservation of empire is the first and foremost of those interests.

Rethink the false narrative that the British have offered to keep you on their side. Do not allow their self-serving fiction to color the decisions you make today.

dacherry3@yahoo.com
ramasimongt@hotmail.com

ships around the cities, new levels of education and literacy were required of them for their work roles in industrial society. The Black lawyers, schoolteachers, clerks, and shop stewards were essential to achieving a revolution on the political plane without a bloodbath.

Rethink the Empire's Narrative

For centuries, the British Empire's policy toward Africa was one of *overt* white "race patriotism," with British cabinet ministers referring routinely to Blacks as "niggers" in their correspondence. By the end of 1948, the empire had jettisoned the public expression of its racial policies while handing power to the National Party, whose racial policies were identical in most respects to those the British had previously enforced, but more systematic and even more cruel. This shift positioned the empire's rulers in London to place the blame for racism exclusively on the white Africans. No longer would the British work through a white government in South Africa.

The empire set up the National Party in power to oppose it and crush it, playing the role of "the friend of the African." The decolonization process was a way of perpetuating colonial rule by other means, and for Africa, the process was led by Andrew Cohen, who became assistant secretary in the Colonial Office in 1943. Decades later, one of Sir Andrew's close associates in the Colonial Office, Ronald Robinson, explained it: "So-called

APRIL 16, 2005

HOW MOST OF TODAY'S ECONOMISTS BECAME ILLITERATES

Science: The Power To Prosper

by Lyndon H. LaRouche, Jr.

This article first appeared in Executive Intelligence Review, *April 29, 2005 (Vol. 32, No. 17).*

This report is about economics as that form of science without which no recovery from the presently onrushing world-wide monetary-financial collapse were possible. However, in science, as in preparing a decent meal, it is necessary to clean the kitchen of noxious debris.

However, the intention of this report is not simply to haul out the garbage. Consider that removal of noxious elements of currently widespread opinion as a necessary attack on certain groups of economists who

"To foster the development of mankind, we must look to improving the conditions under which nations live.

Work must be conceived as a true universal, as what society does to increase its power in and over the portion of the universe which society inhabits. It is that quality of transformation of the society's quality of work, which, in turn, supplies the criteria for defining the universal implication of both the work of the individual, and the individual's appropriate *moral* motivation for that work.

Such is the goal of happiness. . . ."

Scientific discovery transforms society, as it is transmitted to industrial production through the machine-tool process. Top to bottom: Institute of Applied Sciences, Mexico City; Marie Curie in her laboratory; engineering classroom, Bombay, India; installation of computerized machine-tools, Cincinnati Milacron; Ford assembly plant, Hermosillo, Mexico.

Credits: United Nations, YN/—b; AIP Niels Bohr Library; United Nations, —vmb; Cincinnati Milacron; EIRNS/Stuart Pettingel

continue to play the role of charlatans, at public expense. These predatory fellows need to be denounced for reason of the damage they would continue to do to the U.S.A. and other nations through the widespread influence of their deceits upon governments and others. I include this attack on them at the outset of this report, if only as a secondary feature of this report as a whole; I do so, because it would be virtually fatal negligence not to attack those dogmas for what will surely be their increasingly desperate frauds at this time. Unless they are denounced for their frauds, on exactly the issues I pose again here, the damage their erroneous opinions have already caused would not only continue, but worsen.

On this account, back in 1971, I accused many among those influential professors of economics of being "quackademics"; over the decades since then, that has been repeatedly proven to have been not only a correct, but necessary choice of language. In retrospect, it is now clear, that had more people heeded my warnings then, the U.S.A., and the world generally, would not be in the ugly mess it is today.

However, the principal topic which I address here. is the fact that, presently, even honest and otherwise intelligent people in government, business, and academia, simply do not have certain knowledge of a type which is absolutely crucial for choosing competent policies under the present crisis-circumstances confronting our government, businesses, and the general public. The principal topic of this report, is the presently urgent necessity of the study and practice of economics as a science, as essentially a branch of experimental physical science.

Under present circumstances, I am therefore obliged to supplement the memorandum which I have recently addressed to the members of the U.S. Senate and their staffs,* by providing professionals and relevant other persons this paper's concise introduction to what are now certain urgently needed, but usually overlooked principles. In this present report, all matters addressed are subsumed under the need to remedy the general lack of that knowledge which must now guide our republic, and our world, out of the presently onrushing catastrophe.

Up to this present moment of my writing, even most among today's visibly leading economists remain ostensibly ignorant of the most elementary of the systemic errors in their thinking. These are errors shown by their continuing complicity in the past three decades' march down the wrong road, into the swamp of the presently onrushing economic chain-reaction collapse of the world's present monetary-financial system. I present those needed principles of economics as a science which makes clear, that this present collapse would not have been possible, had these professionals and their followers not either ignored, or even defied, the previously well-known principles of that American System of political-economy which defined a durably successful design of modern economy, beginning more than two hundred years ago.

Therefore, given the immediate peril of the world's economy today, the continued influence of the ideology of those misguided economists in the policy-shaping of governments including our own, must be considered the poisonous, habit-forming drug which lured the world monetary-financial system into a form of degeneration which should have been foreseen, or, at least recognized, decades ago, as being a recipe for the kind of state of a general catastrophe which we have actually experienced, more and more, in effects experienced during the recent quarter-century.

Therefore, to overcome the present crisis of our national and the world economy, we must do two things. First, rid ourselves ourselves of those specific kinds of diseased thinking about the subject of economics, which have dominated the U.S.A. and other governments' policy-shaping, and caused the ruin of our economy during the recent three and a half decades. Second, circulate the missing, urgently needed true knowledge of how a successful modern economy works, not only among professionals and businessmen, but, to provide a competent grounding in this essential knowledge, through our secondary schools and universities. The latter, second purpose is the principal concern of this report.

To make those two points in this report, I have chosen the timely example of urgent need to diagnose and cure the present collapse of the auto industry. What was wrong? What should we now do instead? How must we think about economics if we are to succeed in overcoming this challenge? How must we think about a successful rebuilding of both the U.S. and world economy over the coming fifty years and more?

In earlier locations I have pointed out some of the

---

* "Emergency Action by the Senate," April 13, 2005.

essential kinds of related causes, and cures, for the failure of General Motors and other managements today. Here, in this report, I focus on the scientific principles which should be applied, instead of those flawed policies which have caused the present collapse of that industry. On the latter account, I shall direct attention in the body of this report to some extremely relevant, essential principles of economics, principles which were generally unknown to leading economists in universities and elsewhere, up to the point of their study of this report. I supply selected examples of this general ignorance, examples which I choose because they are ones more readily understood among the audience I have selected for this occasion.

I have also pointed, below, to the nature of the still deeper, scientific principles which must govern the way in which we pass down education in the principles of economy from the university level, into the secondary school curriculum, and the public generally.

To speak bluntly, the virtual "brainwashing" of the upper echelons of business leaders and elected members of government on the subject of economy, has carried matters to the extreme, that a crash of enterprises as significant as an entire automobile industry reflects a quality of conditioning which hinders the business executive's or political figure's ability to think rationally about the decisive issues of the crisis of that industry. Typical, in recent years up to the present time, is the case in which the sense of a crisis in the physical economy, prompts the relevant individual's flight from the physical-economic reality of the situation, a flight which is expressed in such forms as rebuking his informant, "But, tell me how the market is doing. . . ."

So, whereas, among relevant trade-union leaders from those industrial categories, the reaction to the presently onrushing collapse of an industry, tends to be rational, healthy, and realistic, the same information presented to the political figure who one might presume represents those trade-unionists' political interests, is too often a change of the subject of discussion, to asking about "the market." That "market" has been the same phenomenon which has continued to suggest that the relevant sector of the physical economy is on the road to prosperity, at the same time that the relevant industry has been preparing to crash. It is that latter kind of avoidance of physical reality rather typical of today's so-called "white collar class," which is expressed by their turning from reality to the subject of "the market"

whenever reality frightens them. That syndrome among them is the most likely influence which might set off the moral failure among politicos which virtually destroys our nation.

A study of the way in which the automobile industry, in particular, has been building up its over-ripeness for the presently onrushing collapse of its relevant corporate institutions, that over years to date, typifies the evidence of the need to shift discussion of the policy-making of our economy from the monetary-financial realm, back to viewing the actuality of the monetary-financial processes from the vantage-point of primary emphasis on the processes at work within the physical economy as such.

That said thus far, the first subject the thoughtful reader should wish to take up now, is the subject of the quality of my expertise. I now preface the body of this report, chiefly, with a few necessary remarks on the most relevant parts, for today, of my background in this field, and after that, turn, in the body of the document, to the crucial point of science to which this report is dedicated.

Some Relevant Personal Background

Often, the instances of either notable success, or ugly failures in the policy-shaping behavior of adult leaders in society, reflect some critical turning-point in development of that personality during childhood or adolescence,

Looking backward from today, it is fairly said that my present career as, in fact, a leading economist, reflects a process which began during my adolescence, in an incident which occurred my first day in attendance at the then standard first secondary school class in Plane Geometry. On that occasion, when the students were challenged by that teacher to suggest why we should study geometry, I volunteered a subject which had fascinated me since some earlier visits to the nearby Charlestown, Massachusetts Navy Yard. I replied to her challenge by posing the subject: *To study why leaving those holes in girders strengthens the structure of which they are a supporting part.* It is the kind of question a boy in my circumstances then would have asked his father. I did ask, but I was never satisfied with the answer he gave me, which was that I should learn the answer in school when the time for that came. School had come, and I had asked.

Despite some prompt, foolish, and also vociferous

ridicule from some classmates on that account, my reflections on what I recognized as their irrational reaction, showed me why I could never accept the idea of a geometry, or physics, premised upon allegedly self-evident definitions, axioms, and postulates of a so-called Euclidean or kindred doctrine in geometry. I never did.

Already, before that classroom incident, I had been prompted by similar questions, to begin a reading of representative writings of leading names in English, French, and German philosophy of the Sixteenth through Eighteenth Centuries. I remained fascinated by that study of philosophies as systems, rather than opinions, from that same standpoint, up through the present day. The pattern of that experience in studying philosophy, initially, during the remainder of my adolescence, showed the significance of that incident in the geometry class to have been, that I was then already on the road to becoming an adolescent admirer of Gottfried Leibniz, over all the other authors of my explorations in those modern European philosophies, These explorations among the history of ideas turned gradually to translations from, and disputed commentaries on the work of the pre-Aristotlean Greeks.

Within two years after that classroom incident, I had become, in effect, a convert to that science of physical geometry which I would come to recognize, more than a decade later, as a Riemannian anti-Euclidean geometry.[1]

The relevance of that seminal classroom incident from my adolescence to this present, brief report, is not only that most professionally trained persons whom I have known from my own, and later generations, developed into adulthood along an intellectual pathway which was systemically contrary to my own. As a result of my adopting the kind of views on geometry which I expressed in that classroom, I have developed what were to be proven to be my superior methods applied to the subject of economy.

So, since my adolescence, my contentious view on the subject of physical geometry, which I had expressed in that geometry classroom, led me to follow the essentially Leibnizian, specifically American track in economics associated with the tradition which Treasury Secretary Alexander Hamilton had identified officially as that American System of political-economy; whereas, most of what passes for generally accepted doctrine, even in the U.S. universities today, is premised on that British East India Company's Anglo-Dutch Liberal school of economy, the doctrine against which the American War of Independence had been fought.

My affinity for the American System, even during adolescence, expressed a non-accidental coincidence with those aspects of my childhood family legacy as a descendant of circles associated with the early Nineteenth-Century American Whigs and their Abraham Lincoln legacy. The outcome of the confluence of that part of family history with the evidence of science, was that I have remained personally comfortable with the agreement between the two influences to the present day.

That experience was the origin of what became my repeated successes as a long-range economic forecaster over decades, during a time when the schools of thought represented by my putative rivals in this field of forecasting have usually failed, often miserably.

Today, the most essential kind of principled significance for science generally, and economics emphatically, of that philosophical difference which I expressed in that classroom incident nearly seventy years ago, can be usefully restated as: *A mere mathematician, such as René Descartes, reports statistically, as did Copernicus, on the motion which has been observed; a physical scientist, by contrast, follows such precedents as Johannes Kepler. The latter not only discovers what has moved the observed object, but bases his presumption and proofs of professional competence on discovering the specific power[2]—the specific universal physical*

---

1. The term "anti-Euclidean," rather than "non-Euclidean," dates in fact from a time prior to the writings of Aristotle or Euclid. It dates in European culture, from the influence of the Egyptian astronomy known as *sphaerics* among the Pythagoreans and Plato. Although a return to "anti-Euclidean geometry" is implicit among Nicholas of Cusa and his principal followers, in physical science, the term "anti-Euclidean" originates with one of the principal teachers of Carl Gauss, Abraham Kästner. The concept is developed, although not under that name, in Gauss's published work, beginning his 1799 doctoral dissertation against D'Alembert, Euler, and Lagrange; but appears, frankly stated, in its own right, with Riemann's 1854 habilitation dissertation and his *Theory of Abelian Functions*. Riemann's conceptions played a decisive role in shaping the development of my own anti-Euclidean notions in physical economy. The term signifies the rejection of *all* notions of "self-evident" (e.g., *a priori*) principles in mathematics.

2. The term *power*, as I employ it here, as distinct from the reductionist's mistaken notion of *energy* as elementary, is the customary English translation of Leibniz's use for science of the German term *Kraft*. Those

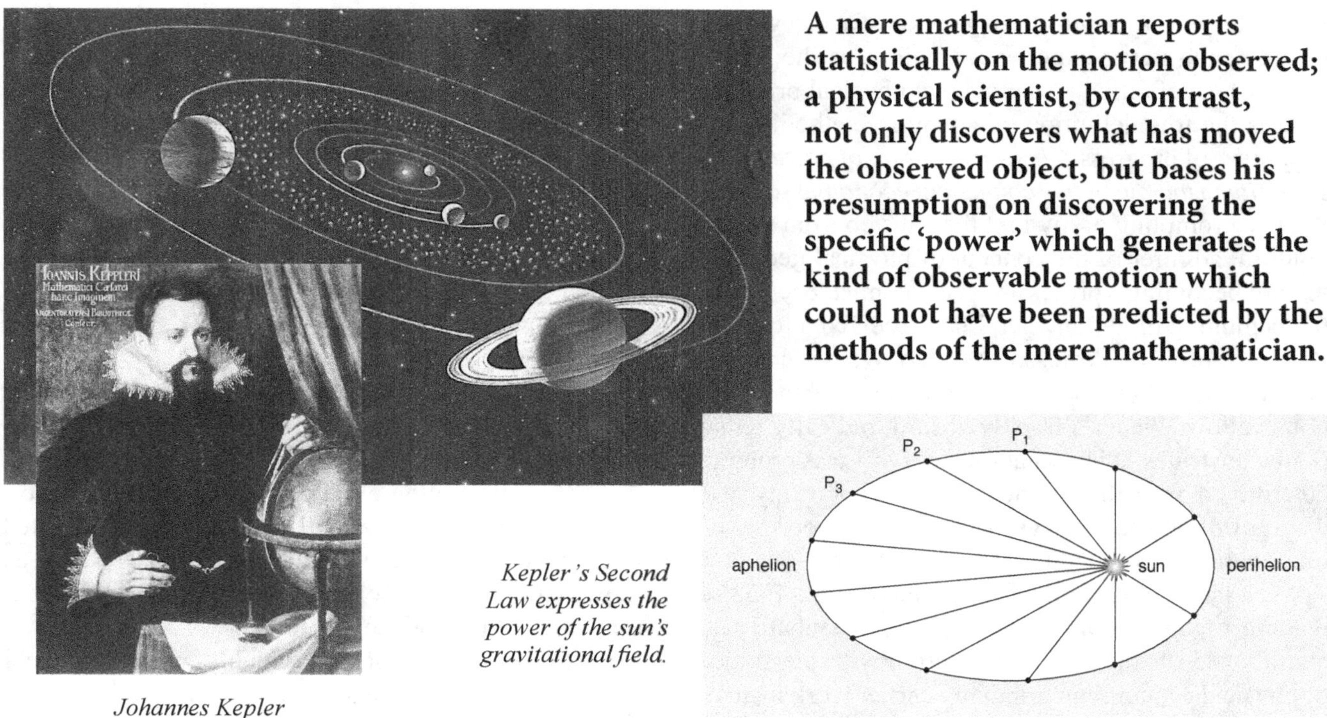

A mere mathematician reports statistically on the motion observed; a physical scientist, by contrast, not only discovers what has moved the observed object, but bases his presumption on discovering the specific 'power' which generates the kind of observable motion which could not have been predicted by the methods of the mere mathematician.

Johannes Kepler

Kepler's Second Law expresses the power of the sun's gravitational field.

principle—which generates the kind of observable motion which could not have been predicted by the methods of the mere mathematician.[3] We observe the movement of the planet. Galileo said that it moves; Kepler asked, and discovered that which moves it.[4]

So, from the beginning of what became my profes-sional successes as a working economist, I had been led to define competent economics, as Leibniz did, as a science of physical economy, whose most characteristic practice is long-range forecasting. The statistician, in his attempted role as forecaster, seeks to predict the movement so; the scientist working in the footsteps of Kepler, Leibniz, Gauss, and Riemann, asks what moves it, *even to produce a state of motion which had never been known to have existed before?* It is the latter sort of motion, forecasting successfully something which had never occurred before, which is inevitably excluded by reductionists' statistical methods, which is the motion which expresses all of those developments which correspond to the most important of all developments. These are the developments which the statistician must necessarily fail to foresee as likely.[5] That discovery of a

terms have the same significance as the use of the term *dynamis* by opponents—such as the Pythagoreans and Plato—of the reductionist schools. The modern form of this Classical Greek usage of the notion of *power*, is traced from such relevant writings as Cardinal Nicholas of Cusa's ***De Docta Ignorantia***, which, with related later writings by him, launched modern experimental physical science along such main lines of development as the direct followers of Cusa, Luca Pacioli, Leonardo da Vinci, Johannes Kepler, and Leibniz. The reaffirmation of this notion of *powers*, against the empiricists' so-called Enlightenment and the followers of Descartes, occurred under the influence, in Germany, of the mathematician Abraham Kästner, Kästner's pupil Carl Gauss, the École Polytechnique of Lazare Carnot, Arago, et al., and the circles of Alexander von Humboldt, which gave us the work of Bernhard Riemann, and the defense of Kepler and Riemann made by Albert Einstein later in his own life.

3. Carl Gauss's discovery of the orbit of the asteroid Ceres, for example.

4. This qualitative difference between Descartes and Leibniz is expressed as systemic in Leibniz's refutation of Descartes on the subject of *vis viva*, where Leibniz's argument reflects the notion of *power* (*dynamis*) adopted, as a principle of what the Pythagoreans and Plato knew as *Sphaerics*.

5. As I have emphasized repeatedly in earlier locations, the typically irrational behavior of the individual and group can be described categorically as a case of a "fishbowl syndrome." The affected individual's reactions are conditioned by a mixture of individual axiom-like assumptions about the universe which limit his or her behavior to the confines of the kind of imagined universe to which those assumptions correspond. That individual therefore "can not see" the larger universe which exists beyond those axiomatic-like assumptions. Thus, the discovery of a universal physical, or kindred principle, frees the mind of the individual to see beyond the neurotic bounds of his own "fishbowl-like"

principle whose application generates a category of phenomenon never experienced before, is the experimentalist's definition of a universal physical principle. That is the true definition of scientific method; that is the *power* of progress. *This same notion of power, is the essential principle of any competent economic science.*[6]

The prompting of my first formal step from being a youthful admirer of the concept of physical geometry, toward becoming a professional economist, occurred at the beginning of 1948, when I had received a loan of a Paris pre-print of Professor Norbert Wiener's **Cybernetics**. Much of that book I found to be fun; but I could not swallow Wiener's frankly absurd, radically reductionist doctrine of "information theory." I was promptly determined, from that moment on, to elaborate my strict disproof of Wiener's cleverly seductive "ivory tower" intervention into economics.

At a later point, during my repeated, 1952-1953 re-reading of the opening paragraphs of Bernhard Riemann's 1854 habilitation dissertation with the subject of physical economy in mind, my earlier work in arriving at a thesis refuting Wiener (and, similarly, John von Neumann) for economics, came into focus. In the leisure imposed by a process of convalescence from a serious bout with hepatitis, I had my "Eureka" experience; I acquired a sure-footed sense of my special competence as an economist, a competence which was later demonstrated in my first general forecast on the economy, which I made several years later, in 1956.

The first working forecast actually made by me on the basis of those studies, which was made during 1956, took shape when I insisted to my rather astonished, and chiefly disbelieving colleagues of that occasion, that we, as consultants to business firms, must foresee a major U.S. recession to erupt approximately February of 1957.[7] That forecast collapse into recession came on time, and for the reasons I had forecast. The effects of my success as a forecaster were much disliked in those circles. Obviously, my doubts of the wisdom of the automobile industry had not caused that recession; but, it is not atypical of the perils of the successful forecaster, that for some associates and others, I must nonetheless be blamed, emotionally, for the effects which reality, not I, had created and delivered to their doorsteps. The typical poor fellow clung to his earlier delusion about the economy, by saying of me, "He talked us into a recession!"

The study which led to my crafting of this forecast had been prompted, initially, by my attention to economically pathological patterns in the marketing practices of leading automobile manufacturers. This observation had turned my attention to broader, correlated other, related factors of virtual fraud by lenders, then, as now, in the misuse of consumer credit by the U.S. economy at that time. Hence, the forecast.

All forecasts of that type which I crafted then, and later, have been premised on the discovery of a characteristically systemic feature of the economic process. Often, as in the case of my 1956 and later forecasts, this systemic feature corresponds to recognition of some influential, usually false, axiomatic-like assumption by some controlling interests in the current system. Like the 1954-1957 process leading into the February 1957 turn, most important forecasts are premised upon a discovered element of systematic delusion of that type, like the "Pyramid Club" frenzy of the late 1940s, or the consumer-financing frenzy leading into the 1957 recession, each of which, like the John Law "bubble" of the early Eighteenth Century, had been induced in relevant mass-behavior.

Then, as in the case leading into the present General Motors crisis, the tendency of the relevant foolish folk is to see apparent short-term monetary-financial advantages in "the market," while putting aside concern for medium- to long-term physical-economic factors. The latter are the factors which will ultimately take their revenge, as now, upon the wishful monetary-financial thinking which has temporarily seduced prevalent opinion.

For example, the fact that the population of the U.S. has been transformed, as a whole, from a nation of savers, into wildly over-extended borrowers, seeing today's money to spend, rather than tomorrow's debt to be paid, is worse than typical of the way short-term de-

---

syndrome.

6. This issue of *power* is addressed directly by Gauss's 1799 attack on the fraud by D'Alembert, Euler, Lagrange, et al., who used the nonsense-word "imaginary" to attempt to conceal the actual, physical existence of the complex domain. The concept of the complex domain, as developed from Gauss through Riemann, is the mathematical form of expression of that ontological principle of *power* as associated with the discovery of uniquely efficient universal physical principles. E.g., Riemann's conception of *Dirichlet's Principle*.

7. My related proposal was that the firm shift emphasis toward getting deeply into the ground-floor of what must be seen as an increasing importance of electronic data-processing in production, distribution, and administration.

lusions of public opinion, lead into medium- to long-term catastrophes. Such are the cases of the 1990s "IT" bubble, the mortgage-based securities bubble, the automobile-sales-financing bubble, hedge funds generally, and the U.S. fiscal debt and current accounts deficit today. In all bubbles, and most boom-bust cycles, there is a systemic element of popular delusion operating axiomatically within induced mass-behavior.

Ironically, we witness the same kind of blunder as then, repeated on a grander scale today, as a key part of the onrushing crash of the automobile industry, and other key sectors. However, while forecasting disasters is not only important, but necessary, it is forecasting ways to bring about a recovery from a presently onrushing disaster, which touches the heart of a scientific quality of professional practice of physical economy. As an illustration of the latter point, take a key feature of my just-issued report on the prospects of a recovery, which I have just issued as a motion presented to the members of the U.S. Senate. This present report is crafted as a technical supplement to that report.

Not accidentally, the systemic error in mismanagement whose effects have exploded to the surface of the world's automotive interest today, was the same type of error, but on a grander scale, speaking of types of systemic errors, which had attracted my attention in the automobile industry of 1956. General Motors' financier management of today has obviously learned less than nothing from the industry's mistakes of fifty years ago.

As I have noted above, my 1956 forecast of a deep 1957 recession had been crafted in a professional capacity as an executive of a firm by which I was employed at that time. However, the study and its specific success prompted a deeper, intense, and far-ranging private study of the trends which I later forecast, beginning 1959-60, as a current trend in our nation's policy-shaping ideology of the mid-1950s. It was clear to me then, that if that ideology were continued in effect, this would set off a series of international monetary crises during the latter half of the 1960s, and, beyond that, presented the added danger of a breakdown of the presently ongoing world monetary system as a result. It actually happened as I had forecast this, over the course of the middle 1960s, through 1971 and beyond. That more widely circulated forecast is that for which I have become known around the world, since the middle to late 1960s. This forecast was realized as the 1967-68 pound sterling and U.S. dollar crises, and the subsequent, 1971-72 collapse of the original Bretton Woods monetary system.

My post-August 16, 1971 statements on this action of the Nixon Administration, which were issued during the remainder of that year, then defined the long-term basis for the series of subsumed, medium-term forecasts, which I later issued at various points during the decades up to that which I delivered through mass media shortly before the 2001 U.S. Presidential inauguration. None of those forecasts of that interval has ever been wrong.

It is the method associated with that general forecast which stands as completely vindicated in the international crises erupting today.

This is not to deny that there are many specialists in various aspects of the economy, who speak with the actual authority of experts in making valid, and sometimes also very valuable statements on the partial significance of current developments. There is often a notable coincidence of opinion between my work and theirs, and some consultation on such matters among us. Nonetheless, my forecasting has the indicated unique quality of significance, as providing the scientific basis for long-term policy-shaping which my success in long-range forecasting expresses. It is the scientific basis for my distinctive successes on that account which must, finally, be learned among those who will be qualified to lead the world into the future, especially those future leaders who emerge from the generation typified by the program of education in certain fundamentals of both science and Classical culture being conducted by my LaRouche Youth Movement.

I work to inform and educate the present leaders from older generations, but also seek to develop a new cadre of leaders of nations who will come to know what I already know far better than I do today. Also, they will still be here to lead in generations which have come to lead after mine has been long gone.

1. What Is Economics?

To discuss the ills and cures of our modern international and national economic systems as such, we must first define what economists and others ought to mean when we use the term "economics." The problem has been, that among presently leading economists or textbooks, very few provide a valid definition for their use

As in the case leading into the present General Motors crisis, the tendency of the relevant foolish folk is to see apparent short-term monetary-financial advantages in 'the market,' while putting aside concern for the medium- to long-term physical-economic factors which will ultimately take their revenge upon the wishful monetary-financial thinking which has temporarily seduced prevalent opinion.

Abandoned GM plant, Danville, Illinois.

EIRNS/Karon Concha-Zia

of the term "economics." Most debates on the subject itself break down at the beginning, turning into a Babel of murky confusion over fundamentals. To avoid that confusion over definitions themselves, I begin my treatment of the technical problems raised by the present General Motors with the following corrected definition of the term economics itself.

The crucial historical fact from which to begin any competent study of economic practice today, is, that no science of economy, in any meaningful sense of the way that term is used today, existed prior to the birth of the modern nation-state in Europe's Fifteenth-Century Renaissance. The first actual economies, otherwise known as *commonwealths*, were founded, successively, by France's King Louis XI and his follower, England's Henry VII, during the Fifteenth Century. Any discussion of the principles which must be recognized, if we are to deal competently with the causes and cure of the presently onrushing, global breakdown-crisis of the world's present floating-exchange-rate monetary system, must begin with an understanding of the scientifically principled differences among the types of European society which existed prior to, during, and after the Fifteenth-Century Renaissance.

The cases of Louis XI's France and Henry VII's England are crucial for sorting out the historical evidence needed to locate the causes and cure for the global crisis expressed by the General Motors and kindred cases today. It would be impossible to grasp what the term sovereign nation-state, or its synonym, the commonwealth, should mean to the competent economist, until the history of mankind, prior to Europe's Fifteenth-Century Renaissance, is seen in a clear-headed way. Until that point is clear, no competent understanding of any the relevant principles of modern economy were possible.

I proceed accordingly.

First of all, although any meaningful definition of the idea of a constitutional republic is traced to the work of Solon of Athens, no actual republic, in that sense, existed in practice prior to crucial developments during the course of the Fifteenth-Century Renaissance. The relevant synonym for a true republic, as founded by France's Louis XI and his follower Henry VII of England, is a *commonwealth; a nation-state whose constitutional law, based on the triple principle of perfect sovereignty, the defense of that sovereignty, and the obligation of society to promote the general welfare of all of the people and their posterity.* The examples are each *equivalent, functionally, to the Preamble of the Federal Constitution of the U.S.A.*, and to the congruent, principled notion of natural law central to the 1776 U.S.

Declaration of Independence, a formulation copied from Leibniz's attack on John Locke's folly, "the pursuit of happiness."

No form of society meeting the standard of that definition existed in any known place prior to that European development of that Fifteenth-Century reform.[8]

This Fifteenth-Century development did not spring up spontaneously. It had developed as an outgrowth of a long process focussed within European civilization and adjoining areas over a period beginning, chiefly, within the geography of Europe and near Asia since approximately 10,000 B.C.

This is the period which began with a catastrophic event, a great flooding, which occurred as a continuation of an already ongoing great melt, which signalled the end of a long period of glaciation in the northern hemisphere. During the whole period of that melt, a process of post-glaciation which had begun more than six thousand years still earlier, there had been a rise in the levels of the world's oceans by approximately three hundred to four hundred feet. These levels, once approximately reached, have defined the general outlines of geography since that point.

This process of post-glacial change had unfolded to the accompaniment of profound successive changes in climate and other contextual factors over the period preceding the events associated with surviving historical accounts, a period of the history of the territory of Europe and Southwest Asia dating from about 4000 B.C.[9]

The way in which European civilization generated the functionally precise conception of the sovereign nation-state, requires us to look at the way in which monotheism shaped that evolving conception of mankind and society out of which the sovereign nation-state emerged in the Fifteenth Century.

The known development of human cultures within the area of Southwest Asia, Africa, and Europe during the approximately four thousand years preceding the birth of Jesus Christ, was the cauldron of conflict, out of which a specific development constituting European civilization emerged, a process of development which came to be centered within what is known today as Classical Greek civilization.

The central factor of that process is birth of mankind's conscious knowledge of a universe and a willful universal deity. The notion of a monotheistic God as a personality conceived as in the image of the mind of man, is a notion buried somewhere deep within the pre-history of the world known to the Egypt of Moses's monotheism. However, the obscurity of the origins of knowledge of the monotheistic principle is not only a feasible challenge; a more rigorous, precise notion of the concept itself, is scientifically necessary. It is essential to focus attention on those creative powers, unique to the human mind among known species, by means of which we are able to sort out clues pointing to the way the human mind, as we know it, could know of the provable existence of such a God. This notion of God, as argued by Plato's ***Timaeus*** dialogue, is the emergent foundation on which the development of European civilization has depended from its beginning.

Typical, for example, is the argument for an actively

____

8. The founding of the modern nation-state by Louis XI and Henry VII was most immediately an outgrowth of the new juridical order in Europe established in the context of the Fifteenth Century's great ecumenical Council of Florence, in which, later, Cardinal Nicholas of Cusa performed an indispensable key role. Two works by Cusa, his ***Concordantia Catholica*** and his founding of modern experimental science with his ***De Docta Ignorantia*** and later scientific works, and his role in launching the policy of great transoceanic exploration and development typified by the actions of Christopher Columbus, were key features of the way in which the immediate conditions for founding of modern nation-states were crafted. The earlier, medieval history of the efforts to establish sovereign states as the replacement for both Roman and ultramontane imperial rule, has been documented from the standpoint of modern international law by Professor Friedrich A. von der Heydte in ***Die Geburtsstunde des souveränen Staates*** (***The Birth of the Sovereign State***) (Regensburg: Druck und Verlag Josef Habbel, 1952). Forerunners of this great Renaissance reform include, most notably, Solon of Athens, Plato, St. Augustine, Charlemagne's opposition to ultramontanism, Abélard, and Dante Alighieri.

9. The reports on ancient astronomical calendars, as this was emphasized by India's Bal Gangadhar Tilak and others, show a highly developed astronomy existing in Central Asia more than 6,000 years ago. Related evidence points to the outstanding importance of maritime cultures based on sophisticated astrogation during times preceding historical times. The evidence indicates that the development of civilization proceeded from the oceans and seas into settlements along principal rivers, rather than the reverse. Traces of settlements along present coastlines, at up to several hundred feet below today's ocean surface, especially where great ancient rivers intersected likely regions, are now submerged, on or near the coastal regions of those ancient times. Therefore, study of relevant, presently submerged off-shore locations, especially off the coasts of India, whose maritime culture of the early historic period played a known important role in the history of adjoining regions, have great importance for our knowledge of the prehistoric conditions of mankind. Such studies would help us greatly to understand the prehistoric development of relatively advanced forms of culture which probably left a crucially significant imprint on the relevant cultures of historic times, such as those of lower Mesopotamia.

creative God by Philo of Alexandria and the Christians, who argued with the same form and degree of exactness we might rightly associate with scientific certainty, rather than some anecdotal blending of legend and chronicles. Plato's *Timaeus*, when situated in the context of the work of the Pythagoreans, and his own dialogues in general, points toward such a scientifically precise knowledge of God and the associated principled notion of society.

Curiously, but not merely coincidentally, Riemann's insight into the implications of Dirichlet's Principle, shows the way in which the human mind can actually know of, and define the notion of an ontological quality of existence of such a monotheistic God with a systematic sense of scientific certainty. As I shall emphasize in the next chapter of this report, all rational notions of science and of modern economy depend upon the ability to conceptualize the notion of a universal principle as a definite, and efficiently ontological object of human consciousness. Riemann's rigorous redefinition of such universals, as stated first in his revolutionary 1854 habilitation dissertation, and as this notion was elaborated in the form of Dirichlet's Principle in his *Theory of Abelian Functions*, enables us, today, to look back with insight to the preceding development of physical science, back to the Classical Greeks, and also, still further, not only to Egyptian astronomy, but notions of astrophysics implicit in Bal Gangadhar Tilak's report on pre-4000 B.C. astronomy in Central Asia.

This elaboration, as by Riemann, of the notion of Dirichlet's Principle, is a crucial quality of modern improvement in our ability to conceptualize those universals which the relevant ancient Egyptians, and the Pythagoreans and Plato, defined as *powers* (i.e., *dynamis*), or what modern Classical science and art know as *universal physical principles*, as absolutely distinct from the merely descriptive quality of mathematical formulas. A clear understanding of this notion, seen in that way, is crucial for defining a notion of economic science, for *a science of physical economy*. This conception is indispensable for achieving a definite, ontological notion of creativity and of the personality of a Creator. This conception is indispensable for understanding more adequately the qualitative specificity of the modern European civilization which first appeared within the context of the Fifteenth-Century European Renaissance.

What we know of the relevant roots of European civilization, is the central role of this idea of a Creator in defining that current which has adopted those special aspects of European civilization as a whole which are relevant for understanding the long struggle, through ancient and medieval times, for the modern birth of the sovereign nation-state republic. Plato's *Timaeus* is the key example of the relevant connections. The conception of man and woman as made in the image of the Creator, all within a continuing process of universal Creation, is the notion which separates Christianity, for example, from the depraved forms of Venetian-Norman-ruled, medieval society from which the revolutionary Fifteenth-Century founding of the modern sovereign nation-state republic largely freed mankind at that time.[10]

That theological conception of man, as typified by such seminal works as Cardinal Nicholas of Cusa's *Concordantia Catholica* and *De Docta Ignorantia*, is the basis for the generalization of both the kind of physical science later typified by Riemann's work, and the notion of man in society. on which the principled organization of the relations among the citizens of a modern European republic is premised. It is the same Cusa, proceeding from the same basis, who led in organizing what became the great explorations across the Atlantic, and from the Atlantic into the Indian Ocean, out of which a modern notion of developing a truly universal civilization emerged.[11]

---

10. Philo is notable for his attack on the fallacy of the Gnostic's syllogism, that if God were Perfect, then his Creation had been Perfect, such that even He could not interfere with a predetermined dramatic script once the Creation had occurred, as the mechanistic, dispensational dogmas of the modern Gnostic Darbyites teach. That Gnostic dogma is also characteristic of the sordid paganism of the cult of the Olympian Zeus of Aeschylus' *Prometheus Bound,* which forbids man's knowledgeable use of the discovery of universal physical principles. Philo's argument on that account, typifies the general method also expressed by competent forms of modern physical science. Creation was not an event, nor a closed drama, but a process of endlessly continuing Creation, in the sense of Heraclitus' famous aphorism as adopted by Plato. The "history" of the evolution of the Solar system out of a fast-spinning, solitary Sun, is an illustration of the point. V.I. Vernadsky's concept of the Noösphere is both an essential conception of physical science, and a theological statement about mankind's role in the organization of our universe.

11. Some of Cusa's writings proposing these explorations fell into the hands of Christopher Columbus. Columbus followed up his study of those documents by Cusa by a correspondence with the scientist and Cusa collaborator Paolo dal Pozzo Toscanelli, who provided Columbus, in 1480, the map which Columbus used in designing the policy for his later voyage into the Caribbean.

Contrary to the doctrines of the empiricists and kindred reductionists, these issues of the history of monotheism are not only theological. They pertain, unavoidably, to those conceptions of man in the universe, man as in the image of the Creator, which also have distinctly secular implications, implications which have to do with the categorical distinction of human beings from beasts. Without understanding the roots of modern European civilization in the notion of man as in the image of the Creator, nothing essential, nothing practical of human existence and modern society could be understood.

The Crucial Conception of Man

This conception of man as a creator in the likeness of the personality of God the Creator, is the essential foundation of both competent physical science and any systemic conception of the modern sovereign state and economy. The most important additional contribution to the development of an integrated view of economy and man as a creator in the likeness of the Creator, was the Twentieth-Century development of the concept of the *Noösphere*, by Russia's V.I. Vernadsky.

Vernadsky, the Russian nuclear scientist and founder of the branch of science known as biogeochemistry, presented to the world his Riemannian conception of the physical organization of the universe, as composed of three multiply-interconnected universal phase-spaces, the abiotic, the Biosphere, and the *Noösphere*.[12] This was premised on crucial experimental evidence showing that the living processes expressed by the production of the relevant fossil aggregations of our planet, were the product of a universal principle not encountered in defining non-living processes, and that the fossil aggregations produced by mankind's discovery of universal principles (the *Noösphere*) were the result of a power not otherwise found among living processes. This latter notion of the term *power* is identical with the original Greek designation as used by the Pythagoreans and Plato, and by Leibniz later.

The implication of that notion of powers is that the universe, like Vernadsky's *Noösphere*, is *a system*. That means a system in the sense that the way in which the universe works is determined by a set of discoverable universal physical principles provided by the Creator.

Thus, to the degree that we discover those universal principles (*powers*) we have gained a partial amount of the total power which the Creator's universe represents.[13]

So, in that way, what we know—or, what we believe that we know of such principles—is also a system, not exactly the Creator's system, but including some part of that. That, of course, leaves us with some errors we have produced, or adopted, and, insofar as what we actually know, leaves much that we have yet to discover.

As the case of Kepler's discovery of gravitation shows, or Leibniz's discovery of what he termed *vis viva* (i.e., powers) which he presented to refute Descartes's blunder, the universe in which we actually live is not a world of our naive sense-perceptions, but a universe of universal physical, and related kinds of principles, which can not be sensed directly, but which we can not only know through experimental methods, but which we can prove, experimentally, are an image of the real universe, where the universe we tend to infer by mere sense-certainty, is only a shadow which the real universe casts upon our senses. The concept of the complex domain, as elaborated by Gauss, Riemann, et al., is typical of the way competent modern physical science represents both the difference and connection between the real universe and the shadow-world of sense-perception.

The characteristic physical-scientific distinction of man from the beasts is this *power* which we associate with discovered universal physical principles, as expressed by the transmission of such discoveries from the sovereign mind of a single individual discoverer to his, or her society, and to future generations.[14] This power of the individual mind, so expressed, is the immortal aspect of the human biological individual, the expression of his, or her participation in the same creative principle which resides in the monotheist's Creator.

It is the notion that we live in a universe ordered by the will of that single Creator, which is the foundation for competent modern science, and is also the moral principle upon which the crafting and existence of the modern sovereign nation-state and its economy depend.

---

12. Cf. Lyndon H. LaRouche, Jr., *The Economics of the Noösphere* (Washington, D.C.: EIR News Service, Inc.) 2001.

13. This is Riemann's then-revolutionary argument in the opening of his 1854 habilitation dissertation.

14. *Ibid.*

Thomas Alva Edison and Charles Proteus Steinmetz, 1922.

EIRNS/Karon Concha-Zia

However, the process of establishment of the modern commonwealth, even up to its present, imperfect form, has been a long struggle, a struggle between the notion of man as made in the image of the Creator, and the contrary view of man expressed by a phenomenon called the oligarchical model of society. Typical of the oligarchical model are the systems associated with ancient Babylon, with Sparta, with the image of the Olympian Zeus, with the Roman Empire, and the medieval ultramontane system under the alliance of the Venetian financier oligarchy with the Norman chivalry. The modern sovereign nation-state, the commonwealth, is a conditional realization of the goal of establishing a form of society consistent with the notion of the human individual as made in the monotheistic image of the Creator. The chief adversary of that conception of man, still today, has been the oligarchical models of society which exist still as outgrowths of the medieval ultramontane tyranny under the Venetian financier oligarchy.

The characteristic of the commonwealth is the transmission of those discoveries of universal physical and congruent principle, from one generation to the next, which is the essential functional, and spiritual distinction of the human individual and species from the beasts. It is the conscious participation in the universal process so defined, which is the unique expression of specifically human *happiness* to which Leibniz and the U.S. Declaration of Independence refer, in opposition to the specific bestiality of John Locke and Locke's pro-slavery followers in the doctrine of "property."

The issue between the republican and oligarchical system is posed, still for today, in the elementary form presented famously by the Classical Greek tragedian Aeschylus' ***Prometheus Bound***. Prometheus is presented there as the advocate of mankind as a species capable of receiving and employing the discovery of those universal physical principles through which man distinguishes his society from that of apes. For that Olympian Zeus, Prometheus' crime was giving usable knowledge of the principle of fire to mankind.[15] It is the denial of the right of human beings generally to have access to knowledge of those universal physical principles typified by ***Prometheus Bound***'s notion of the power of fire, which is typical of the way the oligarchical principle of usury operates as the enemy within a modern commonwealth such as the U.S.A. today.

---

15. The same contempt for the people was expressed in the time following the outlawing of slavery in the U.S.A., by those who insisted that the children of former slaves not be educated above their intended station in life, a doctrine expressed today in such forms as the "no child left behind" doctrine.

The conflict between the interests of the people of the U.S.A. and the financier interests which had savaged the auto industry, is an expression of the conflict between the common good and the principle of financier oligarchy carried over into modern European society as a legacy of the ultramontanism of the awfully ungodly medieval Venetian financier-oligarchy.

The Purpose of Man's Work

The oligarchical concept of man as a subject of the government acting as an instrument of financier-oligarchical power, is that the assigned purpose of man's existence is *work*, a notion of work which is often applied with a vague distinction between the work of the man and of the ox. Work to produce financial and related profit and pleasure for the members of society, especially the owners, and work done to secure the income on which the sustenance and pleasures of individual and family life largely depend.

Those who live on a higher moral plane than that, echo the ***New Testament*** parable of the talent. This is the notion that work must somehow produce some improvement in the condition of life within the society of those who will be living after the doer of that good has passed on, ending life with something equivalent to a smile on his or her face. The principle is that we must make the universe which has "employed" us better for our having lived. Those of us dedicated to that kind of outcome of our mortal existence, spend the entire span of our lives, working to, as it is said, "improve ourselves" as people with an enhanced potential to be useful, that for no other motive than that the opportunity to do so already exists, or could be discovered.

The sublime notion of the purpose of work pertains to a specific distinction of man from beast, the available option of cognitive immortality of the mortal human individual. We are, in that sense, the "fire-bringers" of our society, or, the tool-maker of the automotive plant.

Look at the miserable condition still imposed upon most of the living people of this planet! Is it the meaning of our lives that they and their descendants should live so, or perhaps even worse, over successive generations yet to come? We see more immediately, the wretchedness of the conditions of life by which they are circumscribed. That is the lowest, almost contemptible level of compassion we might experience. Look at the inner misery their circumstances promote. Shall they live, from generation to generations yet to come in that or a comparable condition? Is not the worst betrayal of mankind, and of the Creator, the willingness to leave our fellow-creature in that internally impoverished condition of knowledge and of spirit?

It is the development of mankind, as in the likeness of the Creator, the commitment to do that kind of good, which is the essential form of the work which should motivate us.

Yet, to foster the development of mankind, we must look to the conditions under which nations live. We must improve the planet, and also the Solar system, on that account.

To contribute to those ends, we require relevant conditions of life, for ourselves, as for others. We must therefore produce the improved conditions in our society which make possible that enhancement of the conditions of family life and work itself.

This definition of the notion of work has a reciprocal implication in the uniqueness of modern European civilization, as qualitatively distinct from all known forms of society before it. It is the way in which the notion of work is situated as a systemic characteristic of that new form of society, which supplies us the crucial distinction of modern European society from all known earlier forms of society. It is in this context, this definition of modern civilization as emergent from the Fifteenth-Century Renaissance, that we are rendered capable, as a society, in conquering the immediate challenge which cases such as the crisis of General Motors poses today.

Work must be conceived as a true universal. Work is defined as what society does to increase its power in and over the portion of the universe which society inhabits. It is that universal quality of transformation of the society's quality of work, which, in turn, supplies the criteria for defining the universal implication of both the work of the individual, and the individual's appropriate *moral* motivation for that work, the motivation associated with the individual's *relative satisfaction* with his or her choice of profession, and the society's practical satisfaction with the benefit of that individual's profession.

Such is the goal of happiness, which Leibniz specified in his objection to the inherent bestiality of that notion of "property" (e.g., "shareholder value") admired by Associate Justice Antonin Scalia and others.

That notion, rooted in the concept of true universals,

is the difference which defines the Fifteenth-Century birth of the sovereign nation-state. Instead of society conceived as in congruence with the Olympian Zeus of Aeschylus' *Prometheus Bound*, as the reign of a ruling oligarchy and its appendages, over a mass of human cattle, the emergence of the new form of society, the commonwealth, from the Fifteenth-Century Renaissance, changed the relationship of the individual to society, and, therefore, the notion of work, that in a fundamental way. It is that conception of man, as reflected in the U.S. Declaration of Independence and the Preamble of our Federal Constitution, which is the essential feature of the necessary intention of modern European civilization. It is consciousness of that difference by the institutions of society, and by the individual citizen, *that attitude*, which is the key to the cure of the awful crisis descending upon world civilization at this moment.

2. Work and Its Organization As Power

Mere financial accounting, or the related practice of cost accounting, employs the term *productivity* to refer to a very poorly understood, but perceived effect. Contrary to the accountants and their like, economic science, like related functions of government, must define an increase in productivity as the outcome of the discovery and appropriate application of a universal physical principle, or what we term, in memory of the ancient Pythagoreans and Plato, as *powers*.

The best way to introduce the relevant conception into the modern layman's experience with the increase of the productive powers of labor in society, is to focus on the way in which technological progress, as embodied within the development of basic economic infrastructure, determines the levels of productivity which can be achieved and maintained within both agriculture and industrial and related manufacturing. This connection may be restated, and most simply illustrated, as the interaction with the universal physical principles embodied in basic economic infrastructure, with the universal physical principles expressed in production of physical goods.

The role of *powers* so expressed, is then defined as the distribution of *potential* as Gottfried Leibniz de-fined *potential*. The principal expressions of this distribution of potential are as basic economic infrastructure and as the application of powers in the manner of technology applied to production, or expressed by a product which has been produced for consumption or other use.

This view of *potential*, as the term is associated with Leibniz, brings into immediate view the way in which Carl Gauss and Riemann dealt, respectively, with what I have already identified here earlier in ths report as Dirichlet's Principle.

Take Dirichlet's Principle as addressed implicitly by Gauss in two locations which are most notable examples for our subject-matter here. First, his general treatment of Earth magnetism, and, second, his related collaboration with Wilhelm Weber in defining the experimental principle known as the Ampère-Weber principle of electrodynamics. Contrast these accomplishments in Nineteenth-Century physical science to the reductionists' blunders of the Clausius-Kelvin-Grassmann-Helmholtz-Maxwell circle. See that principle at a higher level of conception, in Riemann's treatment of Abelian functions.

The only discovered manner in which we can deal rationally with the efficient relationship with a universal physical principle, is to express the relevant experimental expression of cause-effect connections in terms of the notion of a *field*. The simplest first approximation of such a representation, is to treat, as Gauss does, the relatively simpler pedagogical problem of defining the distribution of the potential within the interior of an hypothetically circular area, by measuring the potential along the perimeter of that circle.[16] Then, extend that first-approximation illustration of that notion to a multiply-connected Riemannian surface, as Riemann's development of the notion of Abelian functions applies to such cases.

To trace the development of the notion of a *field* in modern European science, revisit Kepler's development of the conception of universal gravitation, as from his **The New Astronomy** through the implications of his **World Harmony**, this time viewing the subject-area treated, in a pioneering fashion, by Kepler, from the standpoint of the work of such as Gauss and Riemann.

---

16. Note that the challenge of mapping a system of higher order relations into the perimeter and interior of a circular area is the first step of pedagogical approach to clarifying the general implications of the notion of Dirichlet's Principle as defined by Riemann.

Look at the miserable condition still imposed upon most of the living people of this planet! Is it the meaning of our lives that they and their descendants should live so, or perhaps even worse, over successive generations yet to come? Is not the worst betrayal of mankind, and of the Creator, the willingness to leave our fellow-creature in that internally impoverished condition of knowledge and of spirit?

Washing from an open ditch, Mexico City.

Then, apply the same approach to the notion of a physical-economic process encompassing a nation, such as the U.S.A., or our planet as a whole.

All discovered, valid notions of any universal physical principle, implicitly define a *field*, a field which is the functional notion of the extension of the efficacy of that principle throughout the universe as a whole. It is the action expressed by the impact of the potential expressed by a field upon the setting in which production occurs, which is the focus of our concern in this report as a whole.

For example, the application of Dirichlet's Principle to any field of action, elevates the experimental viewpoint from a collection of calculations to a single act of conceptual thought, a conception which, like Kepler's notion of universal gravitation, efficiently subsumes, implicitly, all of the relevant, detailed calculations. It is impossible to develop any competent insight into the way a modern economy functions, physically, except by employing the way of looking at a field in the way Riemann's treatment of what he terms Dirichlet's Principle applies.

The understanding of this point which I am developing here, enables us to understand why *the transfer of the production of a product, even when the same technology of design and production is employed, from a developed economy, to a less developed economy, has usually resulted, during the recent quarter century, in a net collapse of the level of the rate of generation of per-capita productivity in the world as a whole!* The transfer of production from a nation with advanced development of its infrastructure, to a nation of relatively poor people with a poor development of general infrastructure, tends to produce a collapse of the physical economy of the planet as a whole. The role of the field represented by basic economic infrastructure, has been ignored, with what tend to become ultimately fatal economic results for all concerned.

By choosing a field of application which itself represents a zone of lower potential, the effective productivity of labor, per capita and per square kilometer, is relatively reduced. By "globalization," for example, the act of production is shifted away from a zone of higher potential, such as the U.S. economy, into a national economy with a much lower potential. Even though the exported technology may be competitive, in and of itself, the effect is usually a lowering of the potential and productivity of the world as a whole, as a result of transferring production from a zone of higher potential to a zone of significantly lower potential.

There is an additional factor to be considered, the order in which advanced technology is applied at various points in the sequence of the productive cycle of the society as a whole. This includes consideration, once again, of the effect of a relatively lowered, or merely unimproved technology of basic economic infrastructure, upon the effective productivity (per capita and per square kilometer) of the relevant economy as a whole. In general, rapid advances in technology in basic economic infrastructure and the machine-tool sector of production, have the optimal outcome for the economy as a whole.

The argument will be made in attempted rebuttal of what I have just written here, that since most people in management and the employed labor-force do not understand what I just said, what I have just written could not, even possibly, be of any relevance to the way production actually works. I reply: "Ignorance is no excuse for the awful results of ignorant management which are expressed in the undeniably actual collapse of General Motors and kindred enterprises today." The field in which production occurs, a field in the sense implicit in Riemann's references to Dirichlet's Principle, is the principal determining consideration in shaping the productivity and growth, or collapse of productivity in a modern economy as a whole.

The rule is, do not put relatively scientifically illiterate persons, such as the typical corporate managements of today, into controlling positions in the economy, including banking, as we have done, increasingly, over the course of the recent several decades of corporate Europe and the Americas.

I treat this matter here in two distinct, but interacting contexts: the way in which basic economic infrastructure defines the variability of potential productivity of the economy (e.g., national physical economy) as a whole, and the way in which the field of application of principle determines productivity in agriculture and manufacturing more directly.

But, also look at the matter of potential in broader terms of reference.

An Example: Leibniz and Bach

Knowing what I know of such matters as that, I prescribed the crafting of the common educational program of the LaRouche Youth Movement on the benchmarks of Gauss's 1799 exposure of the frauds of the empiricist fanatics D'Alembert, Euler, and Lagrange, and, also, the implications of the same type central to J.S. Bach's founding of the principles of Classical musical composition and its performance. The first pole, the implications of Gauss's exposure of the hoax of

Euler et al., pertains to the relationship of the individual human mind to the universe around that individual. The second, Classical musical composition, pertains to the field of the social process, as in Classical modes of choral works, through which the individual acts to effect the cooperation on which the realization of discoveries of physical principles depends.

For example, in the case of Classical composition and its performance, the well-trained, brain-dead musician thinks in terms of chords laid out like a sequences of corpses. The actual follower of Bach's system of well-tempered counterpoint defines the relevant composition as a field in which development of a unity of conceptual effect of the performance of the individual composition as a whole, is located primarily in the more complex modalities of the cross-voice relations of the counterpoint, through which an appropriate unity of effect is achieved.[17] The object is the same as in Riemann's approach to the notion of Dirichlet's Principle, the notion of detail as subsumed by a single, universal conception, a conception, in the case of a relevant Beethoven performance, such as of the Opus 131 or 132 quartet, as a single, essentially individual idea of a principle of composition. The role of the same Lydian progress of cross-voice development met in Mozart's *Ave Verum* as compared with Beethoven's Opus 132, is an example of the unity of a field expressed through a unified process of development according to a principle.

As the famous aphorism of Heraclitus emphasizes, as Plato after him: in the real universe, nothing really exists except constant change. It is the changes in a field, as I have indicated the implications of the term "field" so far here, which are the *efficiently determining* primary reality, rather than, as is often mistakenly assumed, a derived experience.

---

17. For example, what conductor Wilhelm Furtwängler sometimes identified as performing between the notes. In a Classical polyphonic work of many performers, unlike the case of the accomplished string quartet, the individual performing voice does not hear the functional interaction of his or her own voice within the array of voices as a whole. What is heard is the impact of the polyphony upon the volume of the region in which the work is performed and heard. This is heard not as a collection of voices, but as a *field*, as I have identified the notion of a field in reference to the case of Kepler's principal discoveries and Dirichlet's Principle. The exceptionally able conductor, such as Furtwängler, hears the whole in a way which the performers do not, thus seeing and shaping those subtleties which craft the effect of the field of the performed composition, in that acoustical setting, as a sensed indivisible whole.

The same which is to be said of the composition and performance of Classical musical works after J.S. Bach's revolution, is true of all Classical artistic composition, including poetry and drama. In place of Furtwängler's apt use of the expression "performing between the notes," we encounter the often wildly misunderstood terms, poetic, or dramatic *irony*.

The dullard, idiot, or pedant, which are usually only different costumes for the same kind of fool at heart, wishes a net, dictionary meaning, or the equivalent, for every term in the vocabulary used. Not a single competent artist, as composer or performer, would ever do such a disgusting thing as reducing everything to attempted literal meanings, as the unfortunate Associate Justice Antonin Scalia does with his implicitly Satanic dogma of "text." The proper use of words by literate, actually thinking people, is to employ known terms and other images to convey a meaning which the words used have never conveyed on any occasion before that. This reality of Classical irony, too painful to be discussed at a grammarian's funeral, is the typification of the way in which the creative powers of the human mind are expressed in communication.

Only a half-brain-dead pedant could have dreamed of the invention and use of a pseudo-language such as Esperanto as a proposed replacement for living languages of actual peoples living in actual cultures. This was the problem of Latin which Dante Alighieri exposed and remedied by design in the course of defining the pathway to development of the cultures of a sovereign nation-state republic. The same idea, when expressed in one language, can be replicated by appropriate modes applied to a different language; but this translation of actual ideas can not be competently effected by a mechanical process of translation according to standard dictionaries and grammars. The meaning lies not in the words as such, but in the reality to which the words are intended to allude. The music of any use of language lies, as Furtwängler emphasized, "between the notes." In other words, in the ironies of the *field*, as Riemann's reference to Dirichlet's Principle implies.

Take 'Energy,' for Example

Energy, as defined by the reductionist circles of Clausius, Grassmann, and Kelvin, does not actually exist. It is a footprint, not the foot, *power*, which produces the imprint. One important effort to clarify this distinction, was the suggestion that we employ the term "energy-flux density" as a replacement for the crudely scalar notion of "energy" of the usual suspects of reductionism. We used this, for example, in the work of the international scientific association known as the Fusion Energy Foundation. We have used it in our professional practice of economics, to impart a sense of the way in which relatively higher and lower orders of sources of heat-equivalent are ordered as we go up, or down the scale of the ordering of relatively more effective technologies. Thus, we have the ordering of burning of wood, charcoal, coal, petroleum and natural gas, nuclear fission, nuclear fusion, and matter-antimatter reactions as successively higher, relatively more effective, and more efficient orders of technology. These rules of thumb have distinct meanings for practice within the generalities of chemistry and nuclear and sub-nuclear domains of physics. They are in rough, but meaningful correspondence with the notion of a relatively higher, or lower ordering of technologies.

So, in the effort to understand the principled nature of the processes which govern the universe, and its adducible technologies, in the large, we are obliged to plumb into the domain of that which is ever-tinier. To understand the tiniest, we must conceptualize the process in its largest astronomical aspects imaginable, as the paradoxes of the Crab Nebula tease us so. Kepler already thought like that.

The relative weight of power and related potential is greatest in the development of basic economic infrastructure, which should represent about half of the total capital investment by a modern economy such as the U.S.A. Most of this development must occur within the public sector of the economy, rather than private entrepreneurship, just as the achievements of rural electrification show the way in which increased potential over wide areas will have a relatively most powerful multiplier effect on net productivity and quality of product. Improved quality of investment in public education, is among the most powerful multiplier effects, with smaller class sizes (generally not in excess of 15-25 pupils), upgraded goals in technology and Classical culture, and higher ratios of preparation to teaching time for teachers in the system. The advantages of mass transit over individually operated motor vehicles are to be featured, and the organization of territory to minimize travel time, with emphasize on shortening the cost, time, and effort associated with the most frequently required functions of economy and personal life within the territory.

The U.S.A., for example, would benefit greatly, especially over periods spanning a generation or more, from a more dense development of land-areas, such that food supplies are produced locally, as much as possible, and other measures which decentralize as much as possible of the production and services required by each local area and region of the nation, as distinct from the narrowed concentration and process of globalization today.

Virtual "clever idiots" of contemporary corporate management have sought to eliminate actual toolmaking by resort to the brain-dead effects of linearization of design and testing of product through emphasis on computer-synthesis of technologies, with a resulting sharp contraction in the rate of development of power and distribution of potential per capita and per square kilometer in both production and the economy as a whole.

Generally, the higher the rate of turnover effected through technological progress, and the accompanying greater emphasis on science-driven research-and-development as a percentile in the composition of the employment of the labor-force, will provide a relatively optimal effect on productivity in generating and realizing technological progress. The highest rates of benefit come usually from concentrating on the front-end of the process-sheet cycle, in basic economic infrastructure and product and process design, always moving up-scale in what is, in effect, higher energy-flux-densities.

Once we begin to apply the notion of powers and potential to the structure of the national economic process-sheet, it becomes obvious that the U.S.A. today is virtually bankrupt in many respects. The included causes for this effect include the following features of employment and investment patterns.

The composition of employment is way off whack. Much too little employment (and education) in science, engineering, and machine-tool specialties at the front-end of the national production process-sheet. Much too high a ration of so-called "white collar" services employment, relative to so-called "blue collar" employment. Far too low a ration of employment in basic economic infrastructure, especially in the higher technology categories of investment.

The ration of the total labor-force employed in the physical development of basic economic infrastructure is far too low. We must bring investment back up to about half of total employment for combined public and private investment and employment of the labor-force in basic economic infrastructure as a whole. We must get out of emphasis on so-called "soft" technologies, into capital-intensive technologies at the high end of energy-flux densities.

The same general objective stated in another way, is the following.

The general objective of our national reconstruction program must be priority on raising the potential expressed as powers concentrated in the "front-end" of the national process-sheet cycle. The point is to build up the base-line of our national productive potential in the long-term investment cycles associated with the front-end of the cycle represented by the process-sheet of our national economy as a whole. It is the rate of advance of technology (as power, as potential) in this base-line category of the economy, which must have the relatively highest priority, since this affects the base-line of the economy as a whole over the longest period and the broadest base. This is the category in which long-term investment-cycles of basic economic infrastructure are dominant. The complementary area of high priority is the machine-tool sector, as that bridges both basic economic infrastructure and the so-called private sector.

This, which I have just summarized, is sufficient indication of what we must do in the way of changes in investment and budgetary polices otherwise. As recent experience should have shown us, that change is necessary, but is not sufficient by itself. We must rid ourselves of the mental state based on those false but axiomatic assumptions associated with the empiricist premises of modern Anglo-Dutch Liberalism. We must think of a universe which is essentially a system of universal physical principles, a universe in which more and more among us recognize that only those principles associated with the potential of powers are reality in the functional sense of potential, a universe in which we must replace the mechanical way of thinking about economic and related reality, by putting the highest priority on increasing our command of that potential as Riemann's notion of Dirichlet's Principle implies. We must change our ways, to thinking of potential in ways consistent with man as made in his potential as in the likeness of the Creator of our universe.

The Belt and Road Is The Only Answer

by Dennis Speed

Aug. 21—This week's *EIR* refuses to depart from its insistent focus. We will not allow manipulated tragedies, such as the Aug. 12 Charlottesville event, to divert from concentrating our readers on the only road out of what is an otherwise looming potential thermonuclear-war confrontation with Russia, or even with China.

Americans must support this Presidency of the United States by urgently demanding that America join the Belt and Road Initiative (BRI), currently put forward primarily by China and Russia, and to which more than 65 nations are now committed worldwide. Instead of Iraq War-like "coalitions of the willing," the BRI alliance for world economic development is the pathway upward, above war—which has become obsolete for the human race.

While the Belt and Road Initiative is not, currently, the adopted policy of the United States, the BRI is in fact the only way "to make America great": make all of mankind—by improving our productive capacities through a World Land-Bridge— "greater than our destiny." Franklin Delano Roosevelt understood that, and Andrew Young, former Congressman, Mayor of Atlanta, and United States Ambassador to the United Nations, spoke about FDR as a model of how President Trump would have to address the real needs of Ameri-

cans, in a Sunday, Aug. 20 interview on "Meet The Press."

He said, "There is no military solution to almost any problem we face. But there are socio-economic solutions to the problems we face. ... We didn't finally get the world together until 1944, with Franklin Roosevelt, and the United Nations, and the World Bank, and we made sense out of the world, and we created an economy that grew at about six percent annually."

Today, the world, and Americans, should require nothing less from the Presidency of the United States. This Presidency, Young stressed, has that potential: "I think that the thing that the President has to do is think of the American people, all of us, as his family. And I try to think of him as a potential leader, not only of the United States of America, but a leader of the free world and of the enslaved world."

The Trump Administration's presence at the Beijing BRI Forum of May 15, and the Trump Administration's cooperation with Russia in Syria—reversing the Obama Administration's support for "Al-Qaeda" and other British intelligence-sponsored terrorist capabilities deployed to illegally overthrow, or "regime-change" President Assad, have created the basis for the BRI policy to be immediately adopted.

A southwest Asian devel-

LBJ Library Photo/Lauren Gerson

Andrew Young

opment perspective, the Middle East Reconstruction Initiative (MERCI), has been proposed by China, which would welcome the cooperation of the United States, were Presidents Trump and Xi Jinping free to negotiate this. But in what way would this international cooperation be a "win-win" policy for the United States?

Andrew Young's Charlottesville interview opened with him making the observation:

> We [the civil rights movement] originally set out to redeem the soul of America from the triple evils of race, war, and poverty. Most of the issues that we're dealing with now, are related to poverty. But we still want to put everything in a racial context. The reason I feel uncomfortable condemning the Klan types—they are almost the poorest of the poor. They are the forgotten Americans. And, they have been used and abused and neglected. Instead of giving them affordable health-care, they give them black lung jobs. And that just doesn't make sense in today's world.

While Rev. Young, one of the closest and last remaining "young lieutenants" of Martin Luther King, readily admitted that he "didn't know what he would tell the President" to do. However, *EIR* does, in fact, know. *EIR*'s 2014 300-page Special Report, "The New Silk Road Becomes The World Land-Bridge," spells it out for Mr. Young, and all other Americans who want to see a true end to what is erroneously referred to as "racial conflict" in the United States—but without the financial manipulations of Wall Street and the CIty of London.

In embracing the BRI, the United States will immediately be able to return to physical-goods production and advanced agriculture as the primary means of employment of over half its population. The primary and immediate beneficiaries of this re-orientation will be "the forgotten men and women" of the Trump base. The condescending term, "the rust belt," and Hillary Clinton's disgusting "the deplorables," a variation of India's "untouchables," will disappear along with the mass real unemployment that places material progress presently out of the reach of fully one-third of the American population.

The nation will be able to return to the promise of the Kennedy space program through international co-operation with China, Russia, and India, along with Japan and many other countries along the way, in a new science-driven platform of international—indeed extra-terrestrial—cooperation. This would provide the missing substance for Trumps's "jobs for America" good intentions.

This, however, means for America a "reverse cultural paradigm shift," toward physical production at higher skill levels and rates of technological progress. This arrests the deadly policy of "depopulation by de-industrialization" which now directly threatens the lives of half of American citizens, many of whom comprise what is called "the Trump base."

The Dogs of War, and 'Race War'

The danger for British imperial policy-makers, is that their stranglehold on the United States since Nov. 22, 1963 is about to be broken forever. [From] Britain's conflict with the American colonies, escalating immediately following the end of the Seven Years' War in 1763, until November 1963, and [since then] its recent, temporary 54-year "inside job" victory over the Hamiltonian impulse expressed by FDR, might suddenly, unexpectedly be reversed, and end in the Empire's defeat.

What is the British response? To that, the British "cry 'Havoc!' and let slip the dogs of war." Charlottesville, Virginia is about nothing other than that. The "dogs" in Charlottesville, while a different breed, are of the same pedigree as the dogs that today—thanks to Barack Obama's State Department running-dog, neo-con Victoria "F**k Europe" Nuland—roam the streets and parliamentary halls of Ukraine. They also come from the same kennel—the "George Soros Dog Pound." "Black Lives Matter," as several astute African-American commentators have pointed out, is not authentic.

George Soros has financed it with, some say $30 million, some say $100 million. But the neo-Nazis on "the other side" of "Black Lives Matter," use some of the same symbols, including the Confederate flag, that Soros' Ukrainian dogs employ. The Ukrainian dogs are applauded, and lauded, by American media, even as their "white nationalist Neo-Nazi" counterparts in America are denounced.

Barbara Boyd's lead editorial in this issue of *EIR* provides an "ice bucket challenge" to all those that have gotten themselves, understandably, emotionally heated by the tragic, but entirely staged events in Charlottesville. "Entirely staged" does not mean that all the participants agreed to the outcome beforehand, or knew what it would be. Heather Heyer, the young woman who was killed, was a human sacrifice, in the same way that an African-American was hideously sacrificed at California's Altamont Raceway in 1969 during the Rolling Stones' performance of "Sympathy For the Devil." He wasn't personally pre-selected; he was simply there, and "it was going to happen to someone." Heather Heyer was "collateral damage," no more, to the people that staged Charlottesville.

You may choose not to face that, but if, after what you read in both Boyd's articles, on the background of the actors in, and the circumstances surrounding the Charlottesville event, you are still unconvinced, it may be because you are unprepared to do anything about what you now know to be true.

The Next Stage

In any case, a new chapter in the drama is about to commence.

The United States, and the trans-Atlantic monetary system, in early September 2017, is on the verge of a blowout that will dwarf what occurred, or rather, what was no longer able to be hidden by mid-September 2008. The indebtedness worldwide of this system is now at well over $3 quadrillion dollars, perhaps a lot more, and climbing exponentially, twenty-four hours a day.

There is nothing more to loot from the American population—or not enough at least—to any longer maintain the illusion, often repeated, that "the economy is doing really well." Consumer debt has gone as far as it can go. Student individual four-year college loans today are the size of the housing debt fifteen years ago. The auto loan bubble is about to burst.

There is no real American economy to speak of; it has been looted by the City of London, and Wall Street. The purpose of the multiple assaults and diversions, including this latest in Charlottesville, is to prevent the Presidency of the United States from saving the nation and the world by directly issuing credit in the midst of the impending crisis. For that to occur, the Presidency must operate independent of Wall Street, and in opposition to Wall Street's controllers from the City of London, the proximate source of the Russia-Gate hoax, and the primary enemy of the United States.

So, therefore, as in September 2001, expect a "Reichstag fire" scenario, in which one or several inci-dents that are said to be one thing, are actually done for another purpose. In these incidents, people have to die, sometimes in very large numbers, both to give the incidents credibility, and to divert the entire nation from the task that would truly be required to advance the interest of the General Welfare. The United States has been or-dered by its British financial masters—such as the drug-money laundering, terrorist supporting British Hong-kong and Shanghai Banking Corp., usually known today as HSBC bank, a bank protected by the late Obama Administration—to commit suicide. The way the United States will do this, is by going to war with the greatest, most destructive military force in the world—the strategic rocket forces of Russia.

Or, the United States will conduct a stupid, unpro-voked conflict with its greatest ally, the most productive economy in the world, the nation of China.

Know Your Mind to Know Your History

The same forces stoking the fires of racial conflict in Charlottesville, implicitly use the same threat of "the teeming yellow horde" which resulted in the Chinese Exclusion Act of 1881, as the source of emotional dis-trust of the Chinese offer of the BRI today. "Win-Win" cooperation, they say, is "only a propaganda ploy by the Chinese to take over the world."

This is untrue. China is today the greatest proponent of what is sometimes called "the American System," proposed by Lincoln's economic adviser, Henry Charles Carey, author of the book, *The Slave Trade, Domestic and Foreign, Why It Exists and How It May Be Extin-guished.* Americans have not studied Abraham Lin-coln's relationship to China, or Russia's military and other support of the Union against the Confederate cause, including Czar Alexander II's abolition of serf-dom in 1862. Americans don't know the names of Cas-sius Marcellus Clay of Kentucky, Lincoln's Ambassa-dor to Russia, or Anson Burlingame of Massachusetts, Lincoln's ambassador to a still-British colonized China. Both were abolitionists.

In fact, the Chinese Belt and Road Initiative is best understood as the latest attempt to complete the Recon-struction program of Abraham Lincoln, but world-wide—the way that FDR had hoped his new Bretton Woods monetary system and World Bank and United Nations would be the American-modelled cornerstone on which the world itself would be rebuilt, as Andrew Young remembered.

To summarize: The United States has been ordered by its British financial masters, such as the drug-money laundering, terrorist-supporting HSBC bank protected by the late Obama Administration, to commit suicide. The way the United States will do this, is by going to war with the greatest, most destructive military force in the world—the strategic rocket forces of Russia.

Nothing whatsoever that you are now being caused to be concerned about, relative to Charlottesville, has anything remotely to do with the actual imminent threat to your immediate survival posed by the impending destabilization of the Presidency by precisely such staged events as Charlottesville. If the United States does not immediately reverse its policy toward Vladimir Putin and Russia, and if Donald Trump is removed from office through impeachment, or perhaps by the more speedy route of assassination, there will be thermonuclear war with Russia, and you will be unable to do anything to stop it.

The best course is to do what Andrew Young suggested: "Don't get mad—get smart."

It is a good idea to know history. For example, there was no "American Civil War." The somewhat more accurate term, "The War of Secession," is only partially accurate. Lyndon LaRouche has called it "The Foreign-Backed Aggressive War Against the Constitutional Government of the United States." Historian W. Allen Salisbury, author of the now-indispensable book, *The Civil War and the American System*, re-published by *EIR* in 1998, subtitled that work, "America's Battle with Britain, 1860-1876."

Study Salisbury's work, first published forty years ago and intended to prepare Americans for precisely such a moment as this. Andrew Young, standing in for an unavoidably absent Martin Luther King, unfazed by the emotions of the moment, admonished: "We have to keep our eyes on the prize—and the prize is not vengeance, not getting even, but the prize is redemption." Redeeming the soul of America only requires that America remember the minds and the actions of Abraham Lincoln and Frederick Douglass, both of whom exemplified that breaking the mental chains of slavery is the task of all generations, and will ever be, so long as there is to be human progress, and an America in which that progress is to take place.

9 781975 889159